Managing Stress

Acknowledgements

Much of this manual was originally published by PEPAR Publications, and so I am doubly grateful to Willie More of PEPAR for (1) initially having sufficient faith in my work to publish the text; and (2) his generosity of spirit in giving his permission for a new version to be developed and published.

I am also grateful to Professor Jermaine Ravalier for kindly providing the Foreword and to the people who were generous enough to provide the endorsements.

As with all my work, I am very grateful to Dr Sue Thompson who has been so instrumental in keeping me the right side of the line between pressure and stress. Anna Thompson also deserves thanks for her practical support and the very efficient and effective ways in which she delivers it.

I am indebted to the team at Critical Publishing for providing such a fertile environment for developing this new edition in a spirit of producing publications that make a real-life difference in practice.

Practice Manuals
for **Busy**
Professionals

Managing Stress

NEIL THOMPSON

CRITICAL PUBLISHING

First published in 2024 by Critical Publishing Ltd

British Library Cataloguing in Publication Data
A CIP record for this book is available from the British Library

ISBN: 978-1-916925-34-2

This book is also available in the following e-book formats:
EPUB ISBN: 978-1-916925-35-9
Adobe e-book ISBN: 978-1-916925-36-6

Text design by Greensplash
Cover design by Out of House Limited
Project Management by Newgen Publishing UK

Critical Publishing
3 Connaught Road
St Albans
AL3 5RX

www.criticalpublishing.com

Contents

About the author

Neil Thompson is a changemaker who helps individuals and organisations go from surviving to thriving through learning, empowerment and transformation. His powerful insights can make all the difference.

He now runs the Neil Thompson Academy, which provides a wide range of e-learning courses on an annual subscription basis as well as other online learning resources. In addition, the Academy offers Chartered Management Institute qualifications in management and leadership. He also acts as a consultant to Vigoroom, a sophisticated health and well-being platform and heads up the *humansolutions* website, with information and guidance on personal development and well-being.

Neil Thompson

He is an award-winning writer and educator and a visiting professor at the Open University. He has over 300 publications to his name, including 50 books, several of which are best-sellers. His published work is renowned for its ability to explain complex ideas clearly and accessibly without oversimplifying them and to successfully blend theory and practice.

He has qualifications in social work, mediation, training and development, supervision and Management (MBA), as well as a first-class honours degree, a doctorate (PhD) and a higher doctorate (DLitt). He is a Fellow of the Chartered Institute of Personnel and Development, the Higher Education Academy, the International Work Group on Death, Dying and Bereavement and the Learned Society of Wales and a Life Fellow of the Royal Society of Arts and the Institute of Welsh Affairs. He was formerly the editor of the US-based international journal, *Illness, Crisis & Loss.*

He holds a Lifetime Achievement Award from BASW Cymru, the Wales branch of the British Association of Social Workers, and an Ambassador's Award from the Social Workers Union. In 2014, he was presented with the Dr Robert Fulton award for excellence in the field of death, dying and bereavement from the Center for Death Education and Bioethics at the University of Wisconsin-La Crosse.

He has been a speaker at conferences in the UK, Ireland, Italy, Spain, Norway, the Netherlands, Portugal, Greece, the Czech Republic, Turkey, Hong Kong, India, the United States, Canada and Australia.

His website is at www.NeilThompson.info and information about his online presence can be found at linktr.ee/drneilthompson.

Welcome!

… to *Managing Stress.* Stress is a problem of modern life that can have disastrous effects for individuals, families, teams, organisations and beyond.

Unfortunately, a common way of understanding stress is that it is a sign of a weak or inadequate person when, in reality, the situation is far more complex than that. Seeing it in simple terms as just a personal failing neglects the significant role of wider factors and thereby presents a distorted and dangerously misleading picture of the challenges stress presents.

This manual has been developed to help you understand stress more fully and adequately so that you are better placed to manage your own pressures and help others in doing so.

Interspersed within the text are: practice focus examples, highlighted key points that reinforce some of the important messages the manual is trying to get across; tips to help you rise to the challenges involved; and 'reflective moments' to help you reflect on your own experiences and their significance.

The book is part of the *Practice Manuals for Busy People* series designed to help practitioners and managers across a wide range of workplace settings to achieve the best results and to prepare students for a successful career in their chosen field.

Foreword

Stress in the workplace is one of the most important considerations for employers, employees, practitioners, and academics in the UK and across the world. In the UK, stress in the workplace is among the most common reasons for sickness absence across all occupations. In fact, stress is the number one cause of long-term (lasting four weeks or more) sickness absence in the UK, and is second only to colds and flu for short-term sickness absence. The public sector also seems to be more negatively affected by stress-related absence than the private sector, with people in public-facing roles more likely to go off work.

Some of my most recent research has also demonstrated that many of our most important public sector employees, such as NHS staff, teachers, and social workers, are working under some of the most difficult conditions of all occupations in the UK. These working conditions are subsequently adding to the already-high levels of sickness absence in these occupations. Social workers, for example, are consistently exposed to working conditions which contribute to worsened health outcomes, making them less satisfied in their jobs and more likely to leave their role and social work altogether. I therefore have been working with professional organisations, politicians, employers, and employees to improve these conditions. The suggestions made within Neil's new manual can help employers and employees to improve working conditions and subsequently have knock-on effects for organisational outcomes too.

This manual provides some important background as to why stress at work should be an important consideration in organisations. I have often found that employers need a bit of convincing as to the need to positively deal with work stress, and the manual can help with this. It also outlines what stress is and some of the causes – people often misunderstand these concepts, making this again an important element of the book. Finally, the manual goes on to outline sources of support and how employees and employers can deal with stress at work. Again, this is invaluable information.

This manual is therefore a valuable resource for employees, employers, academics, and practitioners alike. Employers and employees can use the suggestions within their organisation to make improvements for themselves and colleagues. Practitioners can use the manual as the basis of their work in improving organisations, and academics as the basis of research aiming to make positive improvements. I will be suggesting the manual to anyone who requires support as a source of information.

Neil – I think this book is an important read for anyone who has an interest in work-related stress and, for that, I thank you.

Professor Jermaine M Ravalier
Buckinghamshire New University

Introduction

Stress is a subject that has fascinated me for many years. The immense pressures that staff can face in meeting both the day-to-day challenges of their work and the more exceptional traumatic incidents that occur from time to time provide a complex backcloth that repays careful study. It is to be hoped that this manual will make it abundantly clear that the various dimensions of stress add up to a situation that merits close attention from all concerned – theorists, researchers, trainers and, perhaps most importantly of all, the managers and practitioners who have to wrestle with the issues on a daily basis.

It has been pleasing to note that, in recent years, more and more organisations and individuals seem prepared to take seriously the problems presented by stress and their implications for staff, managers and other 'stakeholders', although we still have a long way to go before it is given the careful attention it deserves.

This is not to say that organisations in general are aware of the implications of stress as an occupational hazard – that would clearly be an overstatement – but we do at least appear to be moving in the right direction, albeit at a slower rate than I would ideally like to see. This manual is presented as a contribution to that growing awareness and is intended to offer both a better understanding of the complexities and a set of practical steps for responding positively to the problems brought about by occupational stress.

The challenges of stress have been heightened in recent years by the Covid-19 pandemic which presented huge challenges to public services and businesses alike, as well as to individuals, families and communities. So many people were faced with huge disruptions brought about by lockdowns and preventative measures, such as social distancing, losing important social contacts with family and friends, being unable to visit family and friends in hospital or care homes. In addition, of course, was immense grief on the part of large numbers of people, partly through the death of loved ones and partly through grieving for the comforting normality and familiarity of pre-pandemic life and the life-affirming activities that were not possible in the restricted circumstances.

Even when the pandemic was over, the pressures did not end for a significant number of people as a result of job losses, businesses closed down, long Covid-related suffering in terms of health and fitness and many people – children and adults – under considerable pressure to catch up with their education. For many people, especially those who were already struggling with such problems as anxiety and depression, the Covid experience proved traumatic.

In addition to these pressures and concerns were the fear, anxiety and uncertainty generated by not knowing who would survive, who would not, what would happen next and how long it would go on for. It is therefore fair to say that the pandemic and its aftermath have significantly upped the ante in terms of pressure and stress, thereby making a fuller understanding of stress and a stronger commitment to tackling it all the more important and pressing.

A further effect of the pandemic has been the popularity in many places of remote or hybrid working – that is, employees working fully or partly from home instead of in a conventional workplace setting. This style of working was imposed on many employing organisations because of lockdowns and social distance requirements. Many struggled with it, but many found it beneficial because of the flexibility it offered. Many organisations found that productivity was not adversely affected and actually improved in many cases (Bevan and Cooper, 2022). As a result, many have continued to adopt remote or hybrid working, even though it is no longer needed for health and infection prevention reasons. This presents a fresh set of challenges in terms of the potential for stress. Consider, for example, someone who is prone to depression who copes well as part of a supportive team, but who would struggle if working at home and not having day-to-day contact with supportive colleagues. However, by the same token, someone who is annoyed by the behaviour of some team colleagues may actually flourish when working away from what they experience as a negative environment (especially if they previously had a long commute that no longer applies). The remote and hybrid working phenomenon has therefore further complicated the situation in relation to stress.

These developments can be understood as part of a broader picture in which the world of work has been changing significantly in recent years (Cheese, 2021). We have seen a move away from the 'jobs for life' expectation to short-term and zero-hours contracts and the rise of the 'gig economy' – that is, a greater emphasis on self-employment. In addition, perhaps the most significant change has been the rapidly growing use of artificial intelligence (AI), with its potential to replace many current forms of employment.

All these changes increase job insecurity and the potential for the pressures associated with such developments to result in harmful stress. As a counterbalance to this, we have seen a major shift towards greater interest and investment in health and well-being in the workplace (Bevan and Cooper, 2022). While this is very much to be welcomed, the major work changes that have given rise to it continue to be a significant cause of concern in relation to the mental health and well-being of the workforce.

Of necessity, this manual will not provide all the answers, but it should none the less help to develop a sound foundation on which to build a coherent strategy of stress management and workplace well-being.

As I mentioned earlier, much of this manual was earlier published as *Stress Matters* by PEPAR Publications. This new incarnation has added a great deal of new material and reorganised the earlier work (suitably updated) into manual format. Since the original work has been published, I have continued to help people address the problems stress causes (and the problems that cause stress) – through consultancy work and the development of e-learning courses. While I have seen a lot of positive changes, I remain concerned that stress continues to be a major problem in the modern workplace, one that brings with it significant costs, both financial and human.

Good luck in your efforts to make a positive difference in responding to the challenge of stress.

Why a manual?

The word 'manual' comes from the Latin word for hand (as in manual labour, manual dexterity and so on), so a manual is a *hand*book. By 'handbook' what I mean is a set of guidelines that can help in direct practice. It is not the sort of text you might scan through to look for a quote to include in an essay; it is a basis for practice. For students, this means that it is likely to be of more use to you on placement (or in preparing for placement) than in your academic work. For others, it is likely to be of more use to you in reviewing and consolidating your practice than in pursuing any further or higher qualifications. It is about *making a difference*.

But don't confuse the idea of a handbook, in the sense that I am using it here, with a 'procedures manual' or set of instructions. The issues are too complex to be handled in that way. Each chapter provides food for thought and insights from my own extensive experience of managing a great deal of pressure, plus what I have learned from being a manager, consultant, expert witness and educator. I have run many, many training courses about stress and related matters over the years, so that is an awful lot of conversations that I have been able to learn from, an awful lot of unofficial, informal research that has taught me what people struggle with, how things go wrong and, just as importantly, what works well. This manual is therefore a distillation of that learning.

Imagine the manual as a senior colleague whose experience and knowledge you can draw on to help and guide you, but not simply as someone who will tell you what to do or make your decisions for you.

Who is it for?

I envisage five groups of people potentially finding this manual useful:

1. students on placement or preparing to go out on placement;
2. people new to their career, wanting guidance and reassurance as they make the adjustment from new recruit to fully fledged employee;
3. experienced employees in a variety of occupations who want to make sure that they are keeping 'in touch' with practice issues and are not just slotting into habits and set procedures – in other words, it can be a resource to aid reflective practice;
4. managers who wish to make sure that they are well placed to offer guidance and support to the staff they supervise and lead;
5. educators, whether in academic settings or in practice agencies, who wish to use the insights offered here to help the learners they are supporting.

Of course, different groups may use the manual in different ways, but, whichever group you are in, you should be able to make this work for you.

How do I use it?

To get the best out of this manual, I would suggest that you read it through from start to finish fairly quickly to begin with. Then, once you have got a sense of what it is all about, you can come back and study each chapter more closely, making a note of your own views and issues. It would make sense to do this in the order in which the chapters are presented within the manual. However, if there is any reason why you would want to bring forward studying a particular area, then there is nothing to stop you from doing so, provided that you don't forget to go back at some point to any chapters you missed out.

But, please do remember that this is not a textbook just to be read, it is a manual to be *used*, a resource to aid you with your thinking and in developing your own approach. So, please do make sure you give the issues some thought and keep a record of your reflections – otherwise you are just going through the motions, and that won't really help anyone.

1   **Why bother?**

Stress is something that attracts a lot of attention and generates a lot of interest.

But, at the end of the day, why should we bother to get worked up about it? Why should we take time out from our busy schedules to worry about it? What makes it worth the trouble of stopping and taking the time to consider the impact of stress and what we can do about it? This first chapter is about going some way towards answering these questions. It involves looking at why stress is such an important issue and one that we should take very seriously – indeed, one that we neglect at our peril.

The short answer to 'Why should we bother?' is simple: because it causes so much harm. Stress harms people in a number of ways, sometimes in relatively minor ways, but sometimes in very serious ways indeed, with profound consequences. In this chapter, the costs of stress will be considered. We should quickly be able to recognise that stress has very many costs and these can be very significant indeed for all concerned. These can usefully be divided into six categories: physical health costs; mental health costs; relationship costs; effectiveness costs; organisational costs; and financial costs.

PHYSICAL HEALTH COSTS

Stress can have very adverse costs in terms of our health. Stress can make us more prone to illness by weakening the body's ability to cope with infections and so on. It can also exacerbate illnesses that are not directly connected with the stress. This can be in terms of a number of relatively minor ailments – headaches, stomach aches, indigestion, skin irritations and so on – or much more serious complaints, such as heart disease.

PRACTICE FOCUS 1.1

Peter was under immense pressure over a considerable period. His wife, Sarah, knew that there was something wrong. This was because of the string of minor ailments Peter had experienced recently, given that he was normally very healthy, with hardly a day's illness over a period of years.

MENTAL HEALTH COSTS

Again, these can be relatively minor or quite major in their consequences. A general feeling of being ill at ease or 'under the weather' can become commonplace at one end of the spectrum, while serious mental breakdowns can occur at the other. Sometimes stress can lead to a 'nervous breakdown', in the sense that levels of anxiety and distress can become unbearable and get in the way of everyday coping, or people so affected can become so depressed that they cut themselves off from their day-to-day lives, as if they have numbed themselves to the pain. It is also not unknown for stress to lead to suicide or at least suicide attempts.

Another mental health cost is that of 'burnout', a response to stress that will be discussed in more detail in Chapter 9.

PRACTICE FOCUS 1.2

Suki worked wonders in making sure that her team of staff weathered the storm through a very busy period while they were short of staff. It was an almost superhuman effort on her part, and it was a pretty impressive performance by all the team members. However, once the worst was over, and things started to settle down, Suki became increasingly withdrawn and gradually sank into a deep depression. It was as if she had used up all her mental and emotional energy and had nothing left to give.

RELATIONSHIP COSTS

Stress can place an immense strain on relationships. Marriages can break up, friendships can come to an end, and family relationships can be pushed to the limits as a result of one or more people experiencing stress.

Sometimes our response to stress can be one of acting out of character, behaving in ways that we would not do normally – and this can be a source of considerable conflict and tension between partners, friends, relatives, colleagues and so on. Consequently, stress can produce a vicious circle in which we create barriers between ourselves and people whose support we normally rely upon, thus making us even more prone to stress because we are less well supported.

PRACTICE FOCUS 1.3

Pat was usually a friendly, cheerful person, popular with both customers and colleagues. However, whenever she went through a 'bad patch', she tended to change her attitude towards other people quite markedly. She would become quite sullen and withdrawn, giving off clear signals that she was not in the mood for chatting or joking. Some of her colleagues stood by her, assuming that there must be a good reason for her mood changes, but others became increasingly impatient, resulting in a great deal of tension and strained relationships.

EFFECTIVENESS COSTS

In general, people do not work as productively or effectively when the pressures they face are too high (or too low – see Chapter 2). One of the consequences of this is that customers, clients, patients or others who rely on effective work by the individual concerned are likely to lose out when that individual is under stress. The likelihood of mistakes is higher (and the likelihood of noticing and rectifying mistakes is likely to be lower), the quality of work is generally lower, and levels of output can drop significantly when stress is a factor for one or more people in the workforce. Stressed workers can become disengaged, distanced from their work and the satisfaction it can bring, and this too can lead to a vicious circle – the less engaged a worker is, the more prone to stress they become.

PRACTICE FOCUS 1.4

When several members of the Payroll Department were off sick at the same time, the remaining staff were under immense pressure to complete the monthly pay round. This led to a high number of mistakes being made and, consequently, to a higher than usual number of complaints and queries, in turn leading to an even higher level of pressure.

ORGANISATIONAL COSTS

The effectiveness costs will be significant for the organisation concerned but there are also other costs to take into consideration from an organisational point of view. Morale can be low, tensions and conflict high, thus possibly having an effect on industrial relations, recruitment, retention, sickness absence rates, responsiveness to change and the overall reputation of the organisation. A stressed organisation can be a very unpleasant place to work in, and one that others may not want to do business with.

PRACTICE FOCUS 1.5

When Pam was shown around the office before her interview, she was pleased to have the opportunity to meet people and to 'get the feel of' the place. However, she was not so pleased after her tour of the workplace. The atmosphere was very tense indeed and she went into her interview feeling very unsure about whether she wanted to work in what seemed to be such an unhealthy atmosphere. Consequently, even though she was presented with very favourable terms when she was offered the job, she none the less decided not to accept the post.

FINANCIAL COSTS

And, of course, all these costs have financial implications – for the individual in terms of lost earnings, or loss of opportunities for promotion; for the organisation in terms of its earning power and efficiency with regard to the best use of its available resources, particularly its human resources.

PRACTICE FOCUS 1.6

The Board were aware that there was a problem around stress in several parts of the organisation, but they were unsure that the costs of a well-being programme would be justified. However, following a presentation by a consultant, they began to appreciate that an investment in such a scheme could well be justified in the long term and would also have a lot of benefits in the short term.

It should be clear, then, that not dealing effectively or appropriately with stress is a costly business for all concerned, an expensive approach to life at work. This should, then, bring to our attention the importance of taking stress seriously – recognising it as a significant feature of modern organisational life with detrimental effects for the various individuals and groups concerned and for the organisation itself.

Although there may be little point in developing precise measurements of the costs of stress, we should at least be fully aware of just how costly stress can be for the individual worker, the organisation, its clients, customers and other stakeholders.

This should alert us to the importance of investing a degree of time and energy into the following.

- *Preventing stress:* Taking the necessary steps to avoid stress being experienced in the first place, protecting staff from an unreasonable level of pressure. This is the basis of workplace well-being, an important concept to be discussed in Chapter 14.
- *Responding to stress:* Recognising that someone is under stress and doing what is necessary to alleviate the situation. It is perhaps inevitable that people will experience stress from time to time, and so it is important to be able to recognise the 'tell-tale' signs and respond constructively and supportively.
- *Dealing with the aftermath:* Acknowledging that, at certain times, a particular individual may need a great deal of support in readjusting after either a prolonged period of stress or an intensive experience of trauma (a serious incidence of violence, for example).

CONCLUSION

It should be clear that there are some important and pressing reasons why we should 'bother' about stress, why we should take the trouble to address the issues involved. Those organisations (and there are very many of them) that adopt a head in the sand approach and simply hope that stress issues will fade away are treading a dangerous path, as are those that fail to recognise the significance of stress in the first place.

If we are to be well placed to rise to the challenges presented by stress, then we need to be clear about what counts as stress. Unfortunately, there is considerable confusion about this, as the way the terms stress is used in its 'official' technical sense and how it is used in informal conversation can be quite different. It is because of this that Chapter 2 is devoted to establishing clarity about what exactly we mean by stress.

EXERCISE 1

Consider the various costs of stress discussed here. They are clearly significant, and yet so many people fail to take stress seriously.

- What reasons do you feel there might be for that and what could be done to change the situation?

2   What is stress?

The question of 'What is stress?' is in some ways a difficult one to answer, as stress is defined in different ways by different people. Some people regard stress as something that can be positive or negative – in the right quantities it can be good for you, a source of stimulation and motivation, but, where there is too much of it, it becomes a problem and a health hazard. People who use the term in this way would then distinguish between 'stress', which can be positive or negative, and 'strain', which is where the stress has become excessive and is always negative or harmful. An alternative view is that of people who reserve the term 'stress' for the harmful effects of an inappropriate level of pressure, and use the more neutral term, 'pressure', to refer to the demands made on us which can be positive or negative, depending on just how demanding they are. Figure 2.1 illustrates these two approaches to stress.

1 Stress vs strain		
Stress		
o Enough	= Positive	= Stimulation and motivation
o Too much	= Negative	= **Strain**
2 Pressure vs stress		
Pressure		
o Right balance (not too much, not too little)	= Positive	= Stimulation and motivation
o Too much (or too little)	= Negative	= **Stress**

Figure 2.1 *Two approaches to pressure and stress*

There is no need to decide which is the 'right answer' in terms of these two different approaches. For the remainder of this manual, I shall use the terms 'pressure' and 'stress' as explained in Approach 2 above. This is partly for the sake of consistency and clarity, and partly because the second approach recognises that stress can arise because there is not enough pressure as well as when there is too much – a situation I discuss in more detail in Chapter 3.

The second approach also fits better with the legal context, in so far as the Health and Safety Executive define stress as: *'the adverse reaction people have to excessive pressures or other types of demand placed on them'* (HSE, 2024). A key term here is 'adverse' – in other words, stress is being defined as something that harms us in some way (our health, well-being, relationships, confidence, quality and quantity of work and so on). A key question we need to ask ourselves, therefore, when considering whether or not stress is an issue is: Are the pressures involved in this situation causing harm? We shall return to this point later.

🔒 **KEY POINT**

In everyday conversation, people will often say they are stressed, using the term 'stress' very loosely. It is very important that we do not allow such loose usage to lead us into confusing pressure and stress. We need to remember that pressure is a neutral term (it can be positive or negative), but stress, in its technical sense, is always a problem.

There are many examples of how stress manifests itself that can be brought to mind fairly easily. These include the following 'cameos'.

- Tom shows a much higher level of anxiety than usual. He seems permanently 'on edge', not able to relax or unwind. Because he is so tense, he tends to make everyone else around him tense – he just seems to 'exude' stress.
- Denise appears to lack her usual vitality. The spark that usually makes her such a popular member of the team seems to have eluded her, temporarily at least. She seems to be struggling in a way that is very uncharacteristic of her.
- Said is clearly not thriving at the moment. Everything he does is tentative and unsure. His usual calm confidence is far from apparent. He seems very insecure, as if there is something very serious worrying him.
- Jan has always had a good health record, but these days she seems to be on sick leave on a fairly regular basis. It's never anything serious, but she does seem prone to going down with every bug and ailment going around. It's as if she's got no resistance left.
- Paul used to be fairly easy to get on with, but he must be going through a bad time at the moment, because everyone is steering clear of him. People are just fed up with his brusqueness and the aggressive tone that never seems far below the surface these days. He's like a changed character.
- Lisa used to have a great sense of humour, and you could rely on her to cheer everybody up. However, since the last reorganisation, she seems to have lost her spirit altogether. The most you get out of her these days is a polite smile – she seems to have lost her sense of fun.

What these examples should help to illustrate is that stress can manifest itself in a number of forms, often in ways we would not directly relate to stress. Indeed, this is one of the reasons why stress can be so persistent – we do not recognise the patterns soon enough to take preventative steps. This is a theme that will be developed in more detail in Chapter 9.

However, the point worth emphasising at this stage is that we do not need to be experts in stress management to be able to piece together the 'strands' of stress – they are usually fairly easy to recognise once we have begun the process of becoming more sensitised to the presence of stress factors around us, more aware of just how common stress is in our day-to-day lives.

DEFINING STRESS

We have already noted that stress can be defined as the adverse reaction to excessive pressure. Terms like 'adverse' and 'excessive' tell us that stress is a *problem*, it is something to be avoided. It is not, as so many people mistakenly assume, 'good for you'. If we return to our distinction between pressure and stress, we can see that pressure, when it is at a manageable level, can be good for you, but when pressures reach unmanageable or problematic levels, we are in the domain of stress.

> 🔒 **KEY POINT**
>
> It is important, then, that we do not confuse pressure and stress. If we do, we run the risk of failing to recognise the seriousness of the detrimental effects stress can have on individuals, families, teams and whole organisations.

In what has proven to be an influential work, Arroba and James (1987) define stress as 'your response to an inappropriate level of pressure' (p 3). This is an important definition for two reasons:

1. It refers to an 'inappropriate' level of pressure. This does not simply mean too much pressure. It can also refer to too little pressure – when work is too undemanding or understimulating.
2. It refers to 'your response' to an inappropriate level of pressure. Hence, we must recognise that it is not simply the level of pressure that leads to stress, but rather how we respond to that level of pressure. There is a *subjective* dimension to stress. It is worth considering both these points in more depth as they have important implications for how we manage or avoid stress.

INAPPROPRIATE LEVEL OF PRESSURE

Where levels of pressure are 'middling', neither too high nor too low, pressure can be a very positive force. It can have the effect of:

* *Motivating us* – giving us the energy and enthusiasm to keep us going. Pressure is a source of job satisfaction if it comes in manageable chunks.

- *Stimulating us* – keeping us alert and interested, helping us to achieve peak performance or something approaching it.
- *Helping us to learn* – pressure can be a source of learning, a foundation for personal and professional development.
- *Creating a positive working environment* – helping people pull together and support each other in meeting shared obligations and objectives.

However, where pressure is too high, we can experience a range of problems, as the following examples illustrate.

- *Tension and irritability* – which can affect performance, relationships, job satisfaction and so on.
- *Poor health* – minor ailments, exacerbation of existing problems, and, in extreme situations, serious health problems, such as heart disease.
- *Unnecessary mistakes* – through poor concentration, rushing, not thinking things through, and so on.

In short, excessive pressure can lead to the various costs of stress outlined in Chapter 1.

>>> REFLECTIVE MOMENT <<<

Do you recognise any of these 'indicators' in yourself or anyone close to you? If you do, what is this telling you? Being 'stress aware', as we shall discuss later, is an important part of effective stress management.

Where pressure is too low, there are other problems we can experience, including the following.

- *Lack of job satisfaction* – arising from a lack of interest, stimulation and motivation. Boredom arising from too little pressure can mean that there is little or no satisfaction to be gained from work.
- *Unnecessary mistakes* – through poor concentration and/or a tendency to do things in routine ways without thinking about them (being 'on automatic pilot'). Too little pressure can therefore have a similar effect to too much pressure.
- *Deskilling* – caused by not having the opportunity to practise particular skills over a period of time. Instead of becoming more competent over time, a job with too little pressure can mean we actually become less competent as time passes.

However, it should be pointed out that the situation with regard to levels of pressure is not as simple as it might appear. This is because many jobs can involve both too much and too little pressure, depending on which aspects of the job are to the fore (see Practice focus 2.1 below for an example of this). It is therefore possible to switch between too little and too much pressure in the same job – even on the same day in some cases!

Another important issue in relation to levels of pressure is that, ironically, too much pressure can lead to a situation in which there is too little pressure. This is because we can sometimes respond to too high a level of pressure by switching off from it, steeling ourselves against it, as it were. One way in which this can manifest itself is a phenomenon known as 'burnout' (to be discussed in more detail in Chapter 9).

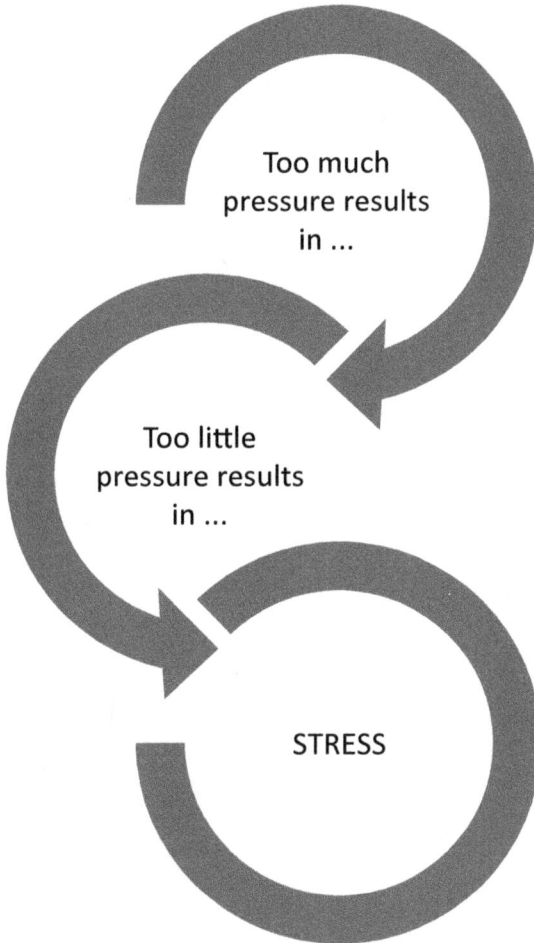

Too much
pressure results
in ...

Too little
pressure results
in ...

STRESS

Figure 2.2 *Too much pressure can lead to too little pressure*

This involves adopting an unfeeling, mechanistic approach to our work, trying to get through the day with the least effort or feeling being expended. Ironically, the result of this can then be a situation in which there is too little stimulation and motivation.

Because we have switched ourselves off from the high level of pressures around us, we can enter a situation in which we actually experience very little pressure. We exchange one source of stress for another.

This process is also very relevant to the question of how we respond to pressure – our subjective response.

THE SUBJECTIVE RESPONSE

The preceding discussion of too much or too little pressure raises the question of what constitutes an appropriate or inappropriate level of pressure. How do we determine what is appropriate and what is not? The short answer is: 'it depends'. That is, it depends on the individual concerned and how he or she perceives the pressure. For example, some people may find a particular event or issue a source of stress, while others find it a way of coping with or alleviating stress. This may be a particular activity, such as gardening, where one person finds it a bind and another pressure to add to the list, while another person finds it a source of relaxation and a means of fending off, or coping with, other pressures. There are no standard responses, no fixed ways of reacting to phenomena – the personal, subjective dimension has an important part to play in determining what is experienced as stressful and what is not.

PRACTICE FOCUS 2.1

Michael was a supervisor in a plastics factory. His main responsibility was to oversee the work of a group of production staff. For the most part, it was an undemanding job. The staff were experienced and reasonably settled in their work, and the equipment being used was modern and generally effective. This meant that Michael was often bored and understimulated, an aspect of the job that sometimes made him think about looking for another job – a more demanding and challenging one. However, from time to time, a problem would occur that demanded urgent and decisive action. Because of the dangerous chemicals involved in the production process, any breaches of work protocol had to be dealt with quickly and effectively if major problems were to be averted. This was a risky and highly pressurised business, and Michael was pleased it did not happen very often. A mistake made during one of these protocol breaches could have very costly consequences. The reality of the job, then, for Michael was a degree of stress from inadequate levels of stimulation for much of the time, with a further and greater degree of stress arising from time to time as a result of a critical incident occurring. In some respects, Michael was exposed to what was, for him, the worst of both worlds.

> ## ! TIP
>
> Beware the common mistake of adopting a 'one-size-fits-all' approach to stress. It is important to be aware that what one person finds very challenging, another person may take in their stride.

CONCLUSION

The term 'stress' is widely used in a very loose sense. People will often say they are stressed when they are under pressure but are actually coping with it. We need to be clear, then, that the sense in which we are using the term 'stress' is more in line with the official Health and Safety Executive definition – that is, using stress to refer to those situations where the level of pressure is *doing harm*.

Whenever you come across people talking about stress think carefully about whether they mean it in the general, loose sense to mean pressure (in which case there is not necessarily a problem involved) or more precisely to mean situations in which the pressures are so great that they are causing problems, potentially very serious problems. It is clearly this latter sense that we are concerned with here.

EXERCISE 2

- In the type of work you are involved with, what are the main sources of pressure?
- In what circumstances might it become possible, or even likely, that the level of pressure will become unmanageable?
- How might you be able to anticipate these circumstances?

3   What causes stress?

This is another difficult question to answer! But it is an important one, none the less. The short answer is that stress can be caused in a number of ways, mainly when our ability to cope, combined with the support we have available to us, are not enough to deal with the pressures we are facing at any particular time. The full answer to the question would be a very long one indeed! What follows, then, is an attempt to find the middle ground between the short and simple answer and the whole picture.

THE STRESS EQUATION

In order to understand how stress comes about, it is necessary to understand the three basic elements of the 'stress equation': stressors (or pressures); coping resources; and support systems or networks. These are the basic ingredients and our understanding of how stress works is based on the interactions across the three below.

Stressors

As we live our lives we become exposed to two sets of stressors:

1. a number of pre-existing pressures, the day-to-day challenges we know about and are used to dealing with; and
2. fresh challenges that arise from time to time – new problems to solve or new situations to adjust to.

Coping resources

In order to deal with the pressures we face, we tend to draw on a range of coping resources. These are skills, methods and strategies that have developed, often over a period of years, and which are used to prevent the pressures from overwhelming us.

Support

How we cope with the pressures we encounter depends, to a large extent, on the nature and extent of support we receive. The absence of support can therefore play an important part in the complex processes through which stress is caused. Coping resources are the subject matter of Chapter 4, where they are examined in a lot more detail. Likewise, questions of support form the subject matter of Chapter 5. The remainder of this chapter is therefore concerned with understanding the role of stressors in causing stress. What exactly are the stressors we face?

🔒 KEY POINT

It is essential that we include consideration of this third dimension. Traditional approaches to stress have tended to present stress as two dimensional, a battle between the stressors (pressures) and our coping (our ability to manage them). This tends to lead to a 'pathological' model – that is, one that blames people for getting stressed (thereby potentially making their stress worse and creating a vicious circle). We shall return to this point below.

COMMON STRESSORS

It has already been noted that stress can arise from either too much pressure or from too little pressure. Too much pressure can arise from having:

- *too much work* – too many tasks to do, or one or more tasks that make considerable demands on our time and energy;
- *work that is too difficult* – tasks that are challenging in some way, for example because they are very complex or make emotional demands upon us;
- *too much change* – too many disruptions to our usual patterns of working, and/or not enough time to consolidate after one change before another one comes along.

Of course, these are not the only ways in which pressure can get out of hand. Other factors that can lead to excessive pressure include the following.

Role stress

Roles are sets of expectations and, as such, can be significant factors as far as stress is concerned. This can apply in a number of ways, each a potential major source of stress:

- *Role ambiguity*: This is where we are not sure what is expected of us, where there is a lack of clarity about what we are supposed to be doing. If we do not know what is expected of us, we cannot recognise our successes or learn from our mistakes, and so job satisfaction becomes very elusive.
- *Role incompatibility*: Some people find themselves in a situation where there is a contradiction between two or more sets of expectations. For example, a supervisor may find that he or she has a conflict between what the staff expect of him or her and what higher management is looking for.
- *Role conflict*: This is similar to role incompatibility but is less clear cut. It refers to situations where people give us mixed messages about what they expect from us – for example, when we behave in a particular way one day and are praised for it, but behave the same way another day only to be criticised for it.

- *Role overload*: At times, we can find ourselves in situations where we have too many roles to fulfil at once, too many plates to keep spinning, as it were. Then, we run the risk of having all the plates come tumbling down as we lose control of the situation.

Lack of support

This is discussed in more detail in Chapter 5, so, for now, all I will do is reiterate the point that we need to make sure that we include this third element as part of a three-dimensional approach, rather than fall back on the traditional two-dimensional approach with its tendency to pathologise people – that is, to see stress as some sort of character flaw, rather than a reaction to a complex, multidimensional set of pressures.

Uncertainty

Working practices have changed significantly over the years, introducing a much higher level of uncertainty and insecurity – short-term contracts, less job security, more people self-employed on a freelance basis, and so on. For those affected in this way, the net result can be elevated levels of pressure.

Poor working relationships

Conflicts and tensions can 'raise the stakes' as far as pressure in the workplace is concerned. Poor working relationships can sour the atmosphere and add considerably to the negative aspects of the work situation. These can arise from personality clashes or conflicts of values or approach to the work. In more extreme cases, such poor relationships can be the result of bullying and harassment.

Organisational culture

Sometimes the everyday patterns and taken-for-granted ways of working can be sources of additional pressure. For example, a 'macho' culture where it is not the done thing to talk openly about worries and concerns can lead to a 'pressure cooker' effect in which the lack of opportunity to talk openly about issues has the effect of stoking up the pressure.

Home–work interface (work–life balance)

There is a complex relationship between home-based and work-based pressures.

These are discussed in more detail below.

Career development

Sometimes, people can be promoted far too soon, with the effect that they struggle to cope with their new job demands. This is often based on the false assumption that someone who does very well at one level in the organisation will be well suited for a post at the next level up in the organisational hierarchy. At the other end of the spectrum, people can find their career advancement plans blocked and therefore feel frustrated, undervalued and unsupported.

Too little pressure can arise from a number of situations, including the following.

- *Insufficient work*: Simply not having enough to do is a characteristic of some types of jobs, particularly those that involve being 'on standby' in some sense – that is, being available in case something goes wrong, but otherwise not being called upon to do anything. In other situations, there may be too little work because of a lack of orders or of demand for that particular organisation's services.
- *Insufficiently demanding work*: Sometimes the work people are expected to do is just too simple or straightforward for them – it does not call upon their knowledge, skills or aptitudes enough. This is often a case of someone being in the wrong job, but the competitive nature of the job market may mean that he or she is unable to get a more demanding job.
- *Routinisation*: Some jobs are, by their very nature, routinised. That is, they involve following a very closely defined procedure or pattern of work. Many production line jobs fall into this category. However, there are other jobs which do not necessarily involve routinisation, but this is something that develops over time, perhaps because the person concerned has been in the job too long and has lost interest. In such cases, we find a form of self-imposed routinisation – what, in my 'Emotional Competence: Developing Emotional Intelligence and Resilience' e-course, I refer to as 'semi-burnout'.
- *Burnout*: This is a phenomenon that is particularly prevalent in the caring professions, but is by no means restricted to them. Chapter 9 considers this problem in more depth but, for present purposes, we should just note that burnout is associated with a lack of pressure and stimulation (generally brought about by an earlier period of excessive pressure, as discussed above).
- *Organisational culture*: Organisations develop patterns of working over time and, with these, come sets of norms, expectations and values. This is what is meant by an 'organisational culture'. Some such cultures are characterised by a low level of stimulation and interest. That is, some organisations have developed a very low-key culture which means that working there is not exactly a dynamic and challenging experience.
- *Lack of confidence*: Sometimes there are many opportunities available for encountering a helpful and stimulating level of pressure, but some staff may not take advantage of these because they lack a degree of confidence in their ability to cope with those pressures. That is, if we are unsure of our ability to deal effectively with certain pressures, we may avoid them, with the possible result that we then become understimulated. Ironically, we then run the risk of entering a vicious circle in which the lack of stimulation feeds our lack of confidence, and therefore makes it even less likely that we will be prepared to take on new challenges.

UNDERSTANDING STRESSORS

Chronic versus acute stressors

Understanding what gives rise to stress is a complex business and has been the subject of many books and research studies. However, we can at least identify some of the main issues that relate to stressors, some of the factors that should help to make sense of the pressures people face. This chapter therefore concentrates on a number of points that should help to cast light on this important aspect of stress management.

An important distinction to draw is that between chronic and acute stressors. The former refers to stressors that endure over a period of time, while the latter refers to those that apply in the short term only. This is partly why the Covid-19 pandemic was so significant in terms of stress – for a high proportion of people, there was no let up from the additional pressures over a considerable period of time. Chronic stressors may include the following.

Chronic stressors

Relationship difficulties

It is not unusual for a difficult or problematic relationship (at work or in our private lives) to act as a source of constant pressure.

Social stigma

Unfortunately, many people are stigmatised in our society (as a result of mental health problems, for example). Consequently, for the people so affected, this can be an ever-present source of problems and additional pressures.

Figure 3.1 *Chronic and acute stressors*

Discrimination

Any single form of discrimination (racism, sexism, ageism and so on) has the potential to serve as a potential chronic stressor, but in combination they can provide immense challenges. For example, an older black woman may have to wrestle with the difficulties brought about by all three forms of discrimination interacting with one another – an example of 'intersectionality' (May, 2015).

Neurodiversity issues

The phenomenon of neurodiversity (which refers to the natural variation in human cognitive functioning and encompasses conditions such as autism and dyslexia) has been receiving greater attention recently. People with such conditions may experience greater sensitivity to sensory stimuli, social interactions, and changes in routine, leading to additional pressures that can contribute to stress. Again, social stigma can add unnecessarily to the pressures.

Poverty

Constantly having to struggle to make ends meet can be draining, physically, emotionally and spiritually. Many people in poverty show immense resilience and somehow manage to cope, but this does not alter the fact that poverty brings huge challenges, not least because of the feelings of alienation that it engenders. As if poverty itself were not enough, the common tendency to stigmatise people at the lower end of the socioeconomic scale adds further pressures that can lead to stress.

Work conditions

Workplaces can have many benefits, but they can also prove detrimental in a number of ways – for example, through bullying and harassment, conflict, alienation and excessive workloads. For many people, the shift towards remote or hybrid working, spurred by the pandemic, has brought significant advantages (greater flexibility and less commuting, for example), while for others it has brought additional pressures – especially for those who do not have home circumstances conducive to work and/or who need the social stimulation of a team around them to motivate them (Fried and Heinemeier Hansson, 2013).

Psychological barriers

Sometimes our own attitudes or psychological make-up can act as additional pressures. For example, if we are too defensive or, at the other extreme, too aggressive, then we may find that we cause additional problems for ourselves. Much of this can be as a result of alienation caused by stigma and/or discrimination.

Acute stressors

Acute stressors may include the following.

A crisis

There may, at particular times, be a crisis that temporarily adds quite considerably to the level of pressure, perhaps tilting the balance to the extent that pressure becomes harmful stress. The modern workplace, with increased insecurity because of the 'gig economy' and short-term and zero-hours contracts, makes crises around employment much more likely, and these in turn can create other crises (for example, by placing additional strain on an already shaky marriage).

Bereavement or other major loss

Grief is a very powerful influence on our thoughts, feelings and actions, and so one or more significant losses can put us under an additional level of pressure. The changing nature of the workplace (Cheese, 2021) means that there is considerable potential for a wide range of work-related losses – for example, as a result of the increased use of artificial intelligence making certain jobs obsolete.

Illness

No one is immune from illness, and what is usually experienced as a manageable level of pressure may suddenly become too much to handle when illness intervenes. Even something relatively minor, like a cold, can be enough to tilt the balance. Of course, the Covid-19 pandemic was a striking example of the detrimental impact that changes in health conditions can make.

Overload

Many people have a fairly stable and predictable workload. However, in some jobs, the level of pressure is far less predictable, and can, at times, become excessive, with the result that stress is experienced for a short time at least. In such times, much will depend on the role of the team. A supportive, empowering and nurturing team can pull together and cope well with the challenges, while a team that does not function well collectively can drive people into 'security bubbles' where each individual team member focuses on their own deadlines and pressures, cut off from team support and solidarity (Thompson and McGowan, 2024).

Financial problems

Inflation and associated cost-of-living crises can mean that people who were previously reasonably financially secure now face significant additional pressures that can leave them very anxious about how they are going to cope and remain solvent, with many people experiencing depression as a result. Financial challenges then morph into mental health challenges.

Home–work interface (work–life balance)

This is the technical term that describes the important interrelationships between what happens in our private lives and what happens at work. Sometimes the two settings can be mutually supportive, but they can also have a very negative and destructive effect on each other. The ideal scenario is one in which both home and work spheres are characterised by appropriate levels of pressure. However, three other possibilities can be found.

1. Work pressures may be at an unacceptable level, but positive home circumstances act as a source of support and solace. Home life can therefore act as a safe haven from the pressures of work.

2. Work pressures may be at an acceptable level, but there are problems at home (for example, family tensions, financial problems). In these situations, work may actually provide some degree of respite from home-based pressures. This is actually a very common phenomenon for a significant number of people.

3. There may be unacceptable levels of pressure both in work and at home simultaneously, leading to a very serious situation as far as stress is concerned. Indeed, it is not uncommon for stressors in the two spheres to make each other worse, thereby setting up a vicious circle, as Practice focus 3.1 illustrates.

The emphasis on remote or hybrid working has thrown these issues into sharp relief. While there are many advantages from being able to work from home all or part of the time – for many people, at least – there can also be additional pressures, especially if the home environment is overcrowded, noisy or otherwise unsuitable, the individual has caring responsibilities and/or there are unhelpful tensions (whether in the family or with neighbours).

PRACTICE FOCUS 3.1

Mohamed worked in a busy office in the financial services sector. Although he earned a lot of money, he had very little job security due to the unpredictable nature of the organisation's business. While he enjoyed his job, he was constantly anxious, as he longed for some degree of security and stability. He recognised that his personality was not really that well suited to this type of work, but was not sure what other type of work he would be able to move into. In his home life, Mohamed was also very unsettled. He and his wife, Marsha, had been considering starting a family for a long time. However, Marsha was getting increasingly keen, and would try to persuade Mohamed that now was the time to stop using contraception. Mohamed was partly in favour of this, but felt that his financially insecure situation was not a good starting point for bringing up a child. He wanted to establish more security in his working life before taking on the insecurities of bringing up a child, particularly as he was not very confident that he would be a good father. However, he was not keen to discuss these issues with Marsha, and so there tended to be a lot of conflict and ill-feeling generated by this situation. She felt he was being immature and not facing up to his responsibilities, while he felt she was being demanding and impatient. The tensions at home made him feel even more insecure and pressurised at work, and these additional pressures made him less willing and able to deal with the problems at home – and the longer the situation went on, the less willing he became to discuss the situation openly with Marsha. A very destructive vicious circle had developed.

> **🔒 KEY POINT**
>
> The emergence of an acute stressor can act as the 'final straw' when it adds extra weight to existing chronic stressors. Similarly, when one or more acute stressors arise at the same time or in quick succession, the result can be an unacceptable level of pressure and thus harmful stress. We witnessed this in relation to the pandemic and, as we have noted, the changing nature of the world of work can be seen to contribute to circumstances in which chronic and acute stressors can combine.

STRESSOR SUBJECTIVITY

The point was made earlier that there is a subjective dimension to stress, in the sense that what one person finds stressful another person could take in their stride. Consider, for example, these scenarios.

- Sam has to deal with an angry person who raises their voice and swears. This leads to considerable distress that Sam struggles to deal with. Chris has a similar experience, feels a little uncomfortable for a little while, but soon gets over it.
- Chris makes a mistake that inconveniences other team members and feels really guilty about it. Chris keeps mulling it over and over and gets quite distressed about letting colleagues down. Sam also makes a mistake that inconveniences colleagues, but simply apologises, makes a joke about it and the whole matter is quickly forgotten.

Such variations in response will depend on a number of factors, such as differences in personality, skill set, experiences of similar circumstances and mood. Much will also depend on the level of other pressures being experienced at the time. For example, someone who is already under immense pressure may struggle to deal with a relatively minor issue that people under lower levels of pressure would cope with in a very straightforward way.

This brings us back to the theme of the shift towards remote or hybrid working. Some people will thrive in such an environment because of the advantages it brings, and they may regard any disadvantages as a small price to pay for the benefits gained. For other people, the disadvantages may far outweigh any positives gained, and so being away from a conventional work base may be perceived as a highly significant stress factor. These are important issues that organisations seeking to adopt remote or hybrid working need to consider carefully if they are not to create significant problems around stress.

One of the key implications of stress having a subjective dimension is that it is important not to make judgements about people based on your own perception. For example, in the first of the two scenarios, if Chris were a manager, there may be a lack of empathy towards Sam, who comes to be seen as not sufficiently robust. Likewise, in the second scenario, if Sam were a manager, Chris could be labelled as oversensitive. Each response needs to be understood on its own terms.

CONCLUSION

This chapter has illustrated some of the many stressors that have the potential to give rise to stress. By distinguishing between chronic and acute stressors, we can understand how a situation that has been manageable for quite some time, despite several chronic stressors, can become unmanageable – and therefore stressful – with the addition of one or more acute stressors at certain times.

We also need to understand that chronic and acute stressors can interact and potentially make each other worse. For example, a person who tends to be unconfident, who is also grieving, can become even less confident, and the lower level of confidence can make it harder to cope with the challenges of grief. A vicious circle can easily develop in some circumstances.

Of course, it has to be remembered that whatever the range, type or combination of stressors we face, it is not these stressors *per se* that lead to stress directly. As we noted earlier, it is our response to these stressors that tends to produce the experience of stress. In order to understand the development of stressful situations, it is therefore necessary to appreciate not only the stressors themselves, but also our responses to them. The question of how we respond to pressure – how we cope – is therefore a crucial one. Consequently, Chapter 4 is devoted to developing a fuller understanding of coping methods and some of the complex issues associated with them.

EXERCISE 3

Think about the stressors you identified in Exercise 2. Think carefully about how they could be categorised as chronic or acute.

- If they fall largely into the chronic category, what additional (acute) stressors might arise at times?
- If the stressors identified in Exercise 2 are largely acute, are there any chronic stressors you hadn't considered?

4   How can I cope?

There are very many ways in which we can cope with the pressures we face, but, as we shall see, not all of them are constructive or helpful. One of the important lessons to be learned, then, rests on being able to distinguish between coping methods that are positive and beneficial and those that are, potentially at least, destructive, harmful and counterproductive. This ability is an essential part of effective stress management, and so we shall look into it in more detail in this chapter. Also important are:

- the distinction between active and passive coping;
- the dangers of having too narrow a 'repertoire' of coping methods; and
- the skills involved in developing coping resources.

We explore each of these in turn.

COPING METHODS: HELPFUL OR HARMFUL?

People cope with pressures in many different ways, and the variety of coping methods available to us is immense. However, it would be a mistake to assume that any coping method is of value. What we have to recognise is that, not only are some coping methods of little use, some are actually quite harmful. For example, some people cope with a high level of pressure by becoming aggressive, taking out their frustrations on the people around them.

This style of coping may work for some people some of the time, but, in general, it can be argued that aggression tends to do more harm than good in a number of ways, for example by:

- generating an equally aggressive response from one or more other parties involved, possibly leading to an escalation of the situation;
- alienating people who could potentially act as a source of support;
- invoking sanctions from an employer or other person in authority who disapproves of the aggressive response (for example, a disciplinary reprimand);
- producing a level of guilt (and thus additional pressure) after he or she has had the chance to cool down.

The benefit of an aggressive response is that it gives vent to pent-up feelings and thus acts as a form of pressure-release valve. However, pressure can be released through more constructive channels, so that the benefits are gained without having to pay the price of aggression.

In addition to acknowledging that some coping methods are generally unhelpful, it is important to recognise that what proves to be an effective and helpful coping method in one set of circumstances can be very problematic and harmful in another. For example, humour can be very appropriate and helpful as a coping method in many pressurised situations, but may be totally inappropriate in others, resulting in embarrassment and further tension. Indeed, the insensitive and inappropriate use of humour in some circumstances can be a source of considerable ill-feeling.

Active versus passive coping

Another important distinction to recognise and take into account is that between active and passive forms of coping. An active coping style is one that seeks to address the problem, to do something about what is causing the stressful situation. Active coping is therefore problem focused. Passive coping, by contrast, does not involve tackling the problem directly, and is more geared towards adjusting to the situation, coming to terms with the pressures faced.

However, we should be wary of falling into the trap of assuming that active coping is necessarily a good thing and that passive coping is not. It all depends on the nature of the problem being faced. Some problems cannot be solved, in which case an active approach may be of very little use, and may lead to additional tensions and frustrations, as our efforts get us nowhere. In such situations, a passive approach may be far more helpful. Learning how to adapt to an irresolvable situation is a wiser approach than generating further frustration and ill-feeling by railing against something that cannot be changed (as a result of a bereavement or other major loss, for example).

By contrast, a passive approach to circumstances that can be resolved or ameliorated may well lead to excellent opportunities being missed, thereby prolonging the stressful situation. Consider the following two examples:

PRACTICE FOCUS 4.1

David was the contracts manager for a large voluntary organisation. He was very concerned and dismayed to find that Social Services had decided to negotiate a contract with another service provider and would therefore not be renewing the contract David had negotiated the previous year. This decision had already been made by the council and was not open to appeal or reconsideration. However, David could not accept this and kept ringing various members of the department, trying desperately to have the situation reconsidered. He became more and more frustrated as time went on, refusing to acknowledge the reality of the situation.

PRACTICE FOCUS 4.2

Nicky was the health and safety officer in a manufacturing company. Changes in the company's policy led to a major increase in her work, to the point where she felt she could not realistically cope with the demands upon her. Her colleague, Sheila, advised her to raise this with her boss and to have the situation reviewed. Sheila was concerned that Nicky was going to make herself ill through worry, and felt that her manager would actually be quite supportive if he were aware of how unrealistic Nicky's workload demands had become. Nicky, however, was not prepared to raise the matter and continued to cope with the pressures in her own way, mainly by finding ways of relaxing and avoiding thinking about work when she was not actually at work. Sheila remained concerned that Nicky was suffering unnecessarily because she was not prepared to take the steps necessary to do something about the problem.

In general, active coping is the most appropriate response to those situations that are within our control or sphere of influence – those that we can do something about. This refers to the problems that we are able to resolve either completely or at least in part. Passive coping, by contrast, is best suited to those situations that are beyond our control, those that, ultimately, we are going to have to accept (see the discussion below of the 'CIA framework').

Another significant aspect of this distinction between active and passive coping is the gender dimension. Research evidence (Matud, 2004) combines with practice experience to confirm that there are significant gender differences in terms of the coping styles that tend to be adopted. That is, men are more likely to rely on active forms of coping, even in dealing with problems that cannot be solved, while women are much more likely to draw on passive coping responses, even where the problems concerned can be addressed. This can lead to problems for both men and women, where they fit their response to their gender rather than to the nature of the problem, as Figure 4.1 illustrates:

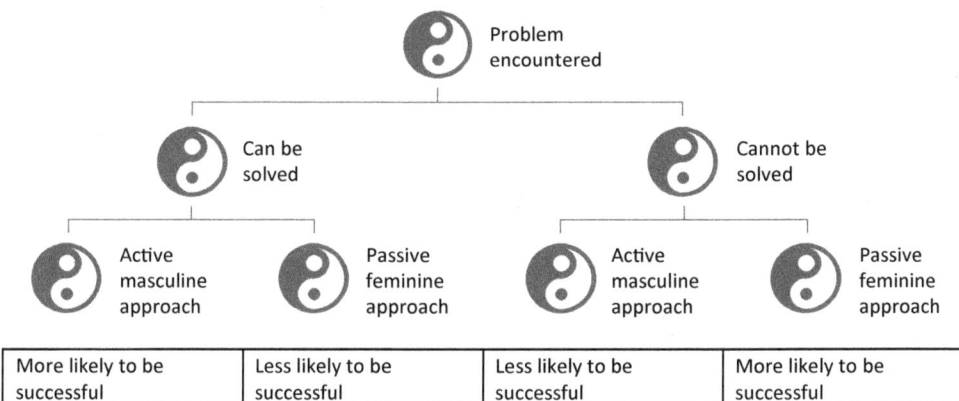

More likely to be successful	Less likely to be successful	Less likely to be successful	More likely to be successful

Figure 4.1 *Active and passive coping*

A repertoire of coping

One important point to note in relation to coping resources is the value of having a broad repertoire of methods to draw upon. That is, we need to avoid having too narrow a range of possibilities for dealing with the pressures we face. This is because a limited range of coping can leave us very vulnerable, as there may be times when these are not available to us when we need them. The more resources for coping we have to draw on, the smaller the chance that we will be caught out without something reliable to fall back on.

The major implication of this is that it is an essential part of any sensible stress management strategy that we ensure that we have a well-developed repertoire of coping methods, that we do not rely on too narrow a range. Consider the following two examples where the people concerned did not incorporate a broad repertoire into their approach to managing their pressures, and take note of the consequences.

PRACTICE FOCUS 4.3

Tom regularly enjoyed drinking sessions with his mates, often having extended sessions at weekends. When pressures started to build up at work, Tom was able to use his drinking as a very effective pressure-release valve. This helped him to cope with considerable pressure during the week. However, as time went on and the pressures continued to grow, Tom found that he was drinking more and more. He started to drink during the week as well as at weekends. This caused a drop in his level of performance at work – which made it more difficult to cope. He had begun to enter a vicious circle. The more he relied on drinking as a coping method, the less well equipped he became to cope. The less well equipped he became, the more he relied on drink. It soon got to the point where the only way Tom felt able to cope was by drinking to excess, and yet this was increasingly becoming the source of his problems. This spiral into drink proved disastrous for him, as he almost completely lost his grip on his life.

PRACTICE FOCUS 4.4

Lisa lived a highly pressurised life, with a demanding job and lots of involvement in charitable work. She coped well with these pressures by regular exercise and involvement in a number of sports. The combination of physical exertion and the sense of achievement provided her with considerable satisfaction and motivation. Her active involvement in sport enabled her to manage a very heavy set of commitments without too much difficulty. However, disaster struck one day for Lisa when she broke her ankle. For several weeks she was not able to engage in physical activities of any kind and it was several months before she was able to return to her previous level of activity. During those months she became very depressed, feeling so helpless without her usual way of coping. She had devoted so much of her time and energy to sports and exercise that she had not left any space in her life for developing other methods of coping. As a result of her injury, her coping strength had deserted her, leaving her very vulnerable.

The message from these two examples should be fairly clear: it pays dividends to develop a broad and varied repertoire of coping methods.

>>> REFLECTIVE MOMENT <<<

Over-relying on one coping method, or at least a very small range, is a very common phenomenon. So many of us are creatures of habit that we can so readily come to rely on a small set of 'old favourites', but this can leave us vulnerable if one or more of them is not available to us at some point. So, it is important that we consider how wide our own coping repertoire is (see Exercise 4).

Defeatism

One characteristic closely associated with stress is that of defeatism. That is, people who are under stress commonly have a tendency to be very negative and cynical, a tendency that so easily leads to defeatism and the mistake of giving up before we have even tried. It is therefore very important to recognise that the negativity associated with stress can make the problem significantly worse. That is, we can easily enter a vicious circle of stress in which we become increasingly negative and defeatist and therefore become reluctant to draw upon particular coping resources, assuming in advance that they will do little or no good. Of course, what happens when we enter such a vicious circle is that we create a 'self-fulfilling prophecy' – our actions (or lack of actions) create the negative situation we anticipate.

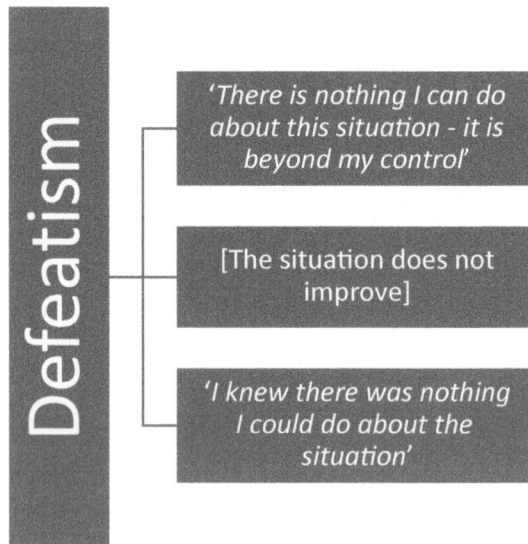

Figure 4.2 *Defeatism as self-fulfilling*

One important conclusion to draw at this stage is that it is vitally important not to allow the negativity associated with stress to drag us down into defeatism and the self-fulfilling prophecy of a vicious circle of stress.

🔴 TIP

Defeatism is often a feature of problematic workplace cultures characterised by low morale, negativity and cynicism, indicative of ineffective or non-existent leadership. To understand the significance of defeatism, we therefore need to look beyond the individual and take account of the wider organisational context.

Least when we need most

One of the great ironies of stress is that we will often cope least at the time we need to do so most. Consider, for example, someone who copes well by listening to music, taking the dog for a walk and having a chat with her best friend on the phone. After a very difficult and demanding day at work she comes home, desperately needing to relax and draw upon her coping resources. However, she may actually be very tempted to settle for letting the dog out into the garden for a little while, putting off speaking to her friend until the following night and not listening to music because 'she can't be bothered'. So, at the time when her coping methods could have been most beneficial, she is least likely actually to use them.

We therefore have to consider how we avoid this problem, as it can leave us very vulnerable to stress. Some helpful steps to consider include the following.

* *Self-awareness*: If we are aware of the process we are starting to go through, we can try to halt it and make the effort to make sure we do not abandon our coping methods.
* *Alternatives*: If we are reluctant to use our usual coping methods, are there alternatives we can draw on, rather than go without altogether?
* *Support*: If others are aware of this tendency, they may be able and willing to support us through this difficult time.

Developing skills

It is important to be aware that coping with pressure and stress is a skilled activity. Many of these skills are what we have developed simply by being effective members of society; other skills may have developed because they are relevant to our job and have become established through training, experience or a mixture of the two. However, no matter how skilful we are now, none of us is perfect; nobody has reached the level of development where there is nothing further to learn, where there are no new developments to benefit from. The consequence of this is that we can all gain from making the effort to develop our coping skills further. It is very difficult to predict how much pressure we are likely to experience at a particular time in the future, and so the more we have 'up our sleeve', the less vulnerable we shall be. One aspect of this can be the trick of turning weaknesses into strengths. This involves looking closely at what aspects of coping we could do with improving (perhaps with the help of a trusted friend or line manager) and working out how these can be turned into strengths – identifying what would need to change to boost our coping skills.

For example, if we find that one problem or weakness is a relative lack of assertiveness (that is, we give in to other people too easily), then efforts geared towards resolving this will not only remove a weakness (being seen as a bit of a pushover by some people, perhaps) but also add a strength in the form of an extra set of coping resources (assertiveness skills and the credibility these bring).

Another important aspect of skill development to consider is that of 'reframing' (or 'cognitive restructuring' to give it its technical name). This involves changing our perspective on, or attitude to, a particular situation or set of stressors. If we can't change the situation, then we can perhaps change our response to it or the meaning that we attach to it. For example, if we are very disappointed by something, we may cope with this by putting it in perspective, playing down how important it was and emphasising other matters that have not disappointed us.

PRACTICE FOCUS 4.5

Tony was very keen to progress in his career and was therefore delighted when an opportunity for promotion arose. He made considerable efforts to impress the senior staff of his company and made a very strong application for the position he wanted. However, when he learned that he had been unsuccessful in his application, he coped with his disappointment by concentrating on how his impressive application and performance had put him in a very strong position in terms of any further promotion possibilities that might arise. He reframed the situation from one of failure to one of success in laying the foundations for a future promotion.

Creative solutions

One characteristic of stressful situations is that we may respond by adopting a 'routinised' approach – that is, by standardising what we do as far as possible in order to create a sense of rhythm and security in what can otherwise be seen as a threatening situation. While this tactic may have some benefits, we must also recognise that it has costs, particularly in terms of building barriers to more imaginative or creative solutions. We therefore have to be wary about allowing the comfort that can be gained from routines standing in the way of thinking more laterally about the problems we face and the potential solutions that can be drawn upon.

A creative approach involves looking at the situation from different angles and seeing whether there are potential ways forward that can be explored. This involves breaking free from following a predefined way of working or an approach with which we feel comfortable. It may well be this 'comfortableness' that is holding us back from finding more innovative solutions by keeping us within the bounds of our usual patterns of thinking and acting.

There are a number of creative coping methods that can be brought into service. If you wish to explore these issues further, you are advised to consult the work of Edward de Bono, a writer who has contributed a great deal to our understanding of creative approaches (de Bono, 1991a and 1991b) – see also Thompson (2024a), which contains 101 problem-solving tools.

The CIA framework

Where we have little or no control over what is happening to us, we are likely to feel vulnerable and insecure, a state of mind that can both be a stressor in its own right and undermine coping resources by affecting levels of confidence. Such insecurity may also make us less likely to seek and use support, thereby exposing us to an even higher likelihood of stress, and potentially plunging us into a vicious circle – a cycle of stress. It is therefore important that the question of control is taken seriously, in both theory and practice. The exercising of appropriate levels and types of control is a central factor in restoring equilibrium so that we do not feel overwhelmed by the pressures we face.

Identifying which aspects of our lives we are able to control can be a significant source of confidence and can form the basis of strategies for managing pressure and preventing stress.

It has to be acknowledged, of course, that there are many factors that are beyond our control. There are many elements over which we have no power and therefore have to come to accept as they stand, however reluctant we may be to do so. This distinction between those factors that we can control and those that we cannot is a long-established one. However, the argument I am putting forward here is that this simple two-way distinction neglects an important issue that lies in between the two extremes of control and acceptance. I am referring to the important role of influence – the attempts, successful or otherwise, to shape events and/or the actions and attitudes of others.

The ability to influence people, events, processes and outcomes is, of course, a central feature of the skills repertoire of many occupational or professional groups.

This ability can be seen as an important factor in rising to the challenge of stress in terms of keeping pressures within manageable limits. In particular, the ability to influence organisations, whether as individual workers or as part of a collective response, can be recognised as a significant element (see the discussion of the 'organisational operator' in Thompson, 2018). Influence therefore occupies an important space between control and acceptance.

Of course, the boundaries between these three elements – **C** for control, **I** for influence and **A** for acceptance – are not always clear and are open to varying interpretations and sometimes subtle processes of negotiation, and are open to change over time, in some respects at least. In addition, our approach to these matters will also tend to vary in accordance with certain psychological factors (level of confidence or self-esteem, for example) as well as sociological ones (the distribution of power according to social location, for example). None the less, the significance of this three-variable conception of coping responses should now be reasonably clear and well established.

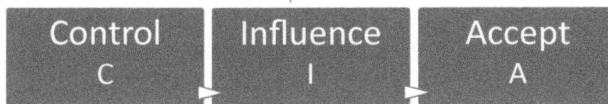

Control	Influence	Accept
C	I	A

Figure 4.3 *The CIA framework*

CONCLUSION

Coping skills come in many shapes and sizes. We all use them, we all benefit from them, and we can all suffer when they are used inappropriately or where they do not match up to the situation we are facing. The benefits to be gained from developing our coping skills are therefore quite significant, and we should take any reasonable opportunity we can to build up our 'repertoire' so that we have a variety of skills and methods to draw upon when we need to.

Of course, coping skills are not enough on their own – they have to be supplemented by effective, well-developed support systems if we are not to leave ourselves vulnerable to stress in the short or long term. It is for this reason that Chapter 5 is devoted to the important topic of using support.

EXERCISE 4

Think carefully about the coping resources you tend to draw on.

- Are there enough of them (is your repertoire wide enough)?
- What additional coping methods might you be able to develop? Are any of your coping methods potentially problematic?
- If so, how can you prevent such problems from arising?

5 Using support

Perhaps one of the most significant barriers to effective stress management is a reluctance to seek or accept support. Once again, there is a significant gender dimension here, with men being far less likely than women to seek support (www.mentalhealth.org.uk/explore-mental-health/statistics). However, the problem is a more general one than this, with both genders significantly represented among those people who, for whatever reason, do not seem to draw upon at least some of the support systems available to them.

SUPPORT SYSTEMS

The issue of support raises a number of important questions, not least the following, which we consider in turn.

1. What support is it realistic or reasonable to expect from an employing organisation?
2. What prevents support systems from being used?

What is realistic?

As a 'bottom line', it is realistic to expect that organisations protect their staff from undue hazards (a health and safety requirement), and it has now become established through legal precedents that stress constitutes a health hazard. Such support systems may include the following.

- *Training and development* – to help equip staff for the pressures they face in their work role so that they are less likely to be overwhelmed by these pressures.
- *Supervision and appraisal* – to provide staff with constructive feedback and advice on how to improve performance, together with guidance and support in terms of on-the-job learning and development.
- *Confidential counselling* – to help staff to explore their thoughts and feelings about the situations they face or have dealt with so that they can be helped to make sense of them and come to terms with them.
- *Grievance procedures* – to enable staff to make formal representations about what-ever they may feel unhappy about, although such formal procedures may create a lot of additional tension and therefore prove counterproductive as far as stress is concerned.

Of course, such formal support systems are likely to be supplemented by more informal support within the organisation (teamwork, camaraderie and so on) as well as informal support outside the work environment (family, friends and so on). We should not forget that trade unions and professional associations can also be major sources of support in many circumstances.

What gets in the way?

While it is clear that there are many potential sources of support, it is also evident, in many organisations at least, that there are several barriers to using such support. These can include the following.

- *Tokenism*, where support systems exist in principle but do not operate in practice (for example, supervision that concentrates too narrowly on accountability issues and fails to address staff development or health and well-being matters – see Thompson and Gilbert, 2019).
- A *'macho' culture*, in which it is assumed that to ask for help is a sign of weakness.
- A *lack of faith* in management leading to mistrust and an unwillingness to rely on management interventions.
- A *lack of awareness* that support systems exist due to a failure to publicise them adequately.
- *Discrimination*, which can apply in two ways. On the one hand, people who are marginalised (for example, on the grounds of gender, ethnicity, sexual or gender identity, disability, language or religion) can receive a lower level of support. On the other hand, fear of being labelled as 'racist', 'sexist' or whatever (what I have elsewhere referred to as a 'walking on eggshells' mentality – Thompson, 2018) can lead to unnecessary tensions that can lead to unhelpful distances between colleagues arising.
- *Remote or hybrid working* can also serve as an obstacle to support. An employee who is working at home much or all of the time and is struggling to cope with one or more sets of pressures may receive no support because the fact that they are struggling is not visible to their colleagues or line manager. It is for this reason that managers of remote workers need to put in place systems for monitoring levels of health and well-being (Thompson, 2024b).

It should be clear, then, that having support systems in place is not enough on its own – there are also steps that have to be taken to ensure that there are no unnecessary barriers to making full and appropriate use of the support available.

UNDERSTANDING SUPPORT

Other important issues in relation to support include the following.

A lack of support leads to people feeling undervalued

When people receive good support, they are likely to feel valued and appreciated – what they have to offer is seen as important, valuable and worthy of support. By contrast, where support is not forthcoming, staff are more likely to feel that they are not appreciated, that their efforts are of little or no value. Such feelings, of course, are then likely to undermine coping abilities and thereby add to the weight of pressure encountered.

Poor or non-existent support tends to become a stressor in its own right

Where there is insufficient support provided or the support is of poor quality, staff may actually find this a source of stress in its own right, rather than a means of dealing with other pressures. For example, unhelpful supervision (what is sometimes referred to as 'snooper-vision') is likely to lead to staff dreading supervision sessions and perhaps avoiding them, rather than welcoming them as a positive source of support.

Support is closely related to levels of confidence

It should be fairly clear that good support has the effect of raising levels of confidence and morale, while poor or non-existent support is much more likely to undermine confidence and contribute to an atmosphere of low morale. Where this persists over a period of time, a 'culture of stress' can develop in which low morale and a lack of confidence in dealing with stress-related problems can become the norm (see Thompson *et al*, 1996).

Destructive or unhelpful support attempts have the effect of 'upping the stakes'

Very poor or inappropriate attempts to support staff can prove to be very destructive, sometimes leading to a vicious circle in which more and more pressure is generated. For example, a line manager dealing with a situation in a very insensitive way can make the experience much worse for the member of staff concerned, possibly leading to a greater reliance on support and thus greater exposure to unhelpful management practices. This can particularly be the case where staff are led to believe that stress is a sign of weakness or personal inadequacy.

A lack of support can lead to feelings of being trapped in an impossible situation

Support is often what staff under pressure rely on in order to get themselves out of difficult situations. Where such support is not forthcoming, it is very easy to begin to feel trapped. Where this occurs, the result can be very problematic, producing either frustration or depression in the short term and either burnout (see Chapter 9) or departure from the job in the longer term.

One-sided support helps with some aspects of the work situation, but not with others

Sometimes staff can receive very good support in relation to one or more aspects of their job, but not in others. For example, a member of staff may feel well supported in matters relating to their current duties, but feel disgruntled at not receiving any support in relation to their future development. They may feel that all that matters to their employers is getting the job done in the short term, with little or no investment of time, effort or other resources in personal or professional development.

Without support, the work–life interface may lead people to take problems home and bring other problems to work

What is often difficult for people is the accumulation of pressures from both the home sphere and the work environment. While each set of pressures may be manageable in their own right, the combination of the two may be overpowering. Support systems can therefore be put to good use in helping to manage the 'interface' between home-related pressures and problems and those arising from the work context. For example, a member of staff may need help in setting boundaries between home and work so that the two can be kept separate up to a point and therefore managed more easily.

Different people have different support needs

Returning for a moment to our earlier discussion of the subjective dimension of stress, we can follow the same logic and appreciate that there will also be subjective differences in terms of what is perceived as supportive. For example, some people may need practical support, others may benefit from emotional support, while yet others may need both. There can also be a need at times for spiritual support – whether or not of a religious variety – for people who, for whatever reason, feel they are losing their way in life.

Supportive solutions don't necessarily cost money

While it can be argued that the investment of resources in effective, well-developed staff well-being systems is a very worthwhile one (see Chapter 14), it should also be recognised that many forms of support are very cheap to implement or have no cost implications at all. For example, a constructive and supportive ethos within an organisation does not necessarily rely on a vast input of financial resources. Often all that is needed in many cases is a commitment to taking stress seriously and the political will to make employee wellness a reality rather than just a rhetorical slogan.

SUPPORT AS THE KEY THIRD DIMENSION

I made the point earlier that traditional two-dimensional approaches to stress run the risk of pathologising people – that is, of reducing stress to the sign of a 'weak' individual. This is because, if we consider only the stressors and the coping methods, this complex situation gets reduced to a simple battle between stressors and coping.

- If the coping methods are strong enough to resist the stressors, stress will not be experienced – coping ability wins out over the pressures. The individual is deemed strong enough to cope.
- If the stressors are too great for the coping methods, stress will be experienced – the stressors win out over coping ability. The individual is deemed too weak to cope.

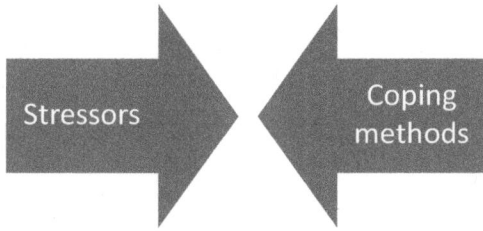

Figure 5.1 *The two-dimensional model of stress*

In this simplistic two-dimensional model, stress is presented as the sign of a weak or inadequate individual. Little or no attention is paid to the wider context or the crucial role of support.

Things change drastically when we introduce the third dimension of support.

- The *presence* of support: (1) reduces pressures, putting them into perspective; and (2) enhances coping ability (for example, by boosting confidence). It therefore has a *doubly positive* effect.
- The *absence* of support (or poor-quality/inappropriate support): (1) increases pressures (due to feelings or resentment, insecurity and so on); and (2) undermines coping abilities (by increasing a sense of vulnerability, for example). It therefore has a *doubly negative* effect.

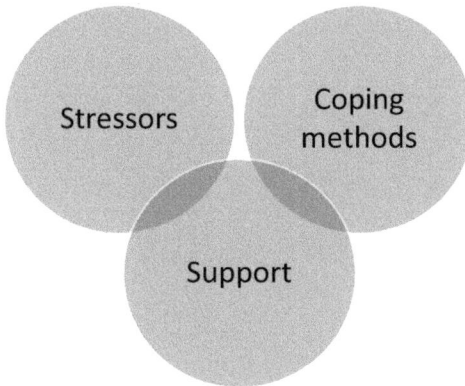

Figure 5.2 *The three-dimensional model of stress*

CONCLUSION

It should be clear from the discussions in this chapter that support is a central aspect of any effective system of dealing with stress. Without support, other efforts to cope with the immense pressures that organisational life so often generates can be doomed to failure or at least seriously undermined. Basically, the notion of 'support' means that we are in this together, that the efforts to prevent, deal with and get over stress should be collective efforts, with a shared responsibility for trying to make sure that pressures are kept within manageable limits.

As support is such a central feature of meeting the challenge of stress, we return to this topic in Chapter 13, where we focus more explicitly on what people within organisations can do to support one another and contribute to a positive and constructive ethos in which stress is recognised as an organisational problem and not simply a sign of personal inadequacy or weakness.

EXERCISE 5

- What support can you rely on?
- Making a list can be reassuring or, conversely, can highlight the need to increase the range of support available to you.
- If the latter is the case, what can you do to increase the potential support you could call upon if needed?
- You might find it helpful to think in terms of both formal and informal support.

6   Avoiding stress

'Prevention is better than cure' is a well-known adage, and also one that applies to stress matters. There are indeed many steps that can be taken to minimise the chances of pressure overspilling into harmful stress. In some respects, a number of chapters in this manual could come under the general heading of 'avoiding stress'.

- Chapter 10: Becoming assertive: It is important that we do not allow ourselves to get into situations where we are being exploited or where our own needs and interests are being ignored.
- Chapter 11: Handling conflict: Violence and aggression are significant sources of stress and so learning how to avoid them is also a means of learning how to avoid stress.
- Chapter 12: Time and workload management: Making sure that we do not become overloaded and do not waste precious time or resources is also an important means of fending off stress.
- Chapter 13: Supporting each other: Support is a crucial factor in keeping work and other pressures at manageable levels.

This chapter does not repeat the ideas to be found elsewhere in the manual but, instead, concentrates on other important issues that have a part to play in avoiding stress.

MAINTAINING CONTROL

The question of 'control' is a fundamental one in dealing with stress matters. This is because an absence of a sense of control can, in itself, be a significant source of stress through:

- an undermining of confidence;
- a higher level of anxiety or depression; and
- a tendency to be negative and defeatist.

It is therefore very important that we are able to exercise as much control as we reasonably can over our circumstances.

In order to do this, we first have to be able to understand what we have control over and what we do not. A helpful model that can assist us in doing this is what I earlier referred to as the CIA framework. This has nothing to do with America's Central Intelligence Agency. What it does in fact stand for is:

C = Control: There are many aspects of our lives that we have direct control over.

I = Influence: There are many other aspects of our lives that we do not have direct control over, but which we can none the less influence – we can have a say in what happens (or at least try to).

A = Accept: There are many things that we cannot control and over which we have little or no influence. These are the things we have to learn to accept, to come to terms with them.

By applying this framework, we can gain an overview of the various aspects of our life and the demands we face. We can identify what we are able to control so that we can go ahead and control them – making sure that we use this control to keep our pressures within manageable limits.

By identifying those factors we can influence, we can decide how best to use our influencing skills (see Chapter 10) to avoid stress – trying to make sure that the pressures we face are not allowed to overspill into harmful stress.

Those elements that we can neither control nor influence then become identified as the ones that we have to accept. Trying to change what we cannot change is, of course, a recipe for considerable frustration, and therefore an additional unnecessary layer of pressure. It is not uncommon for people under stress to lose confidence and therefore underestimate how much control and influence they have – to play down how far they are able to shape what happens and how they respond to it. This can then lead to a degree of defeatism, a negative or cynical approach which tends to lead to inaction and missed opportunities to tackle the problems.

This can lead to a vicious circle, as illustrated in Figure 6.1.

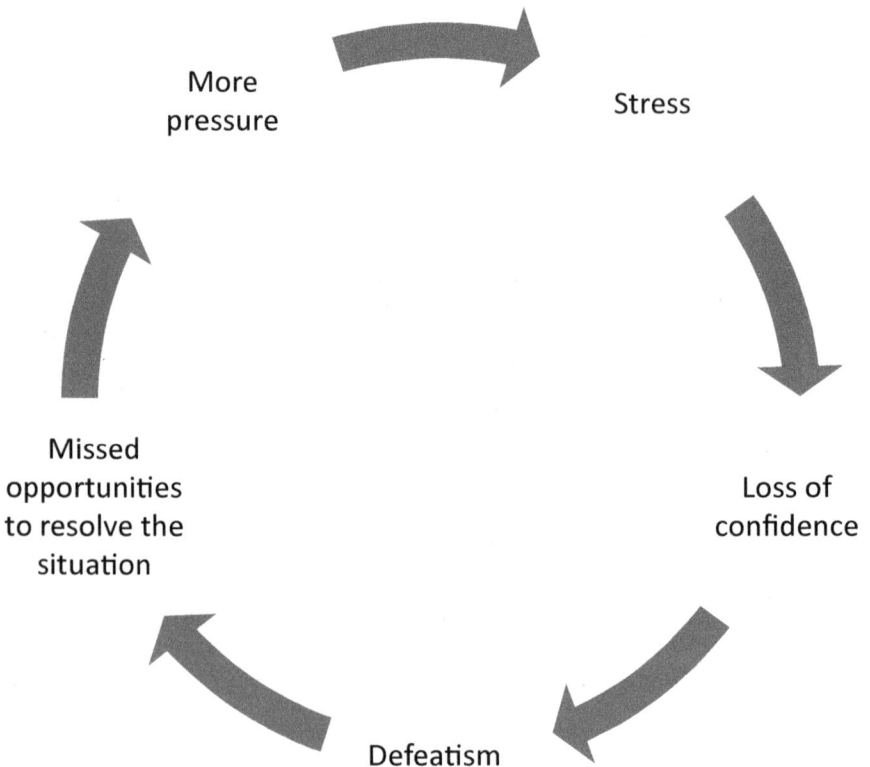

Figure 6.1 *Vicious circle of negativity*

Appreciating, and where possible increasing, our levels of control and influence is a fundamental element of effective stress management – and one that is worth investing in.

SELF-AWARENESS

Stress is not an illness. It is a response to an inappropriate level of pressure. There is therefore a subjective dimension to stress. This means that self-awareness has a part to play – the more we are aware of how matters affect us and how we respond to them, the better equipped we are likely to be to deal with them (see Thompson, 2021, Chapter 1). By developing our level of self-awareness, we can:

- identify what pressures are likely to 'get to us' or cause more than their fair share of problems;
- note where and when these pressures are likely to arise so that we can either avoid them or at least be prepared for them;
- recognise the telltale signs of stress so that we are aware of stress when it affects us;
- understand the range of coping methods available to us, which ones we feel comfortable with and which ones may prove problematic for us;
- explore the range of sources of support that we can potentially draw upon – both formal and informal ones; and
- recognise potential barriers to seeking support when we need it (see Chapter 5).

ORGANISATIONAL AWARENESS

It should be clear, then, that a degree of self-awareness should be a basic requisite for fending off stress. However, we should also note that a degree of organisational awareness can pay dividends. This involves developing an understanding of the following.

Who's who in the organisation?

Who can be relied on for help or support? Who has power and influence? Who may cause me problems or difficulties? Who am I likely to come into conflict with?

Sources of pressure

Where does the potential for stress come from? Are some areas high-pressure places? Are some aspects of the organisation safer than others? Do some people offload their pressures on you?

The unwritten rules

Organisations develop a 'culture' of unwritten rules as well as written ones. It is important to know what these are to make sure that we do not break them without realising that we are doing so. Often breaking an unwritten rule can cause as much of a problem as breaking a written one.

Hidden agendas

While organisations have official agendas in the form of strategies, mission statements, corporate plans and so on, it is not uncommon for individuals or groups to pursue their own agendas. It can pay to be aware of what these are so that we do not fall foul of them.

Potential alliances

Who shares my views and values? Who can I team up with to tackle common problems? Where does the potential for mutual support lie? What can I do to encourage a collective response to problems and pressures?

Control and influence

What aspects of the organisation are you able to control and what aspects are you able to influence (as discussed earlier in this chapter)? By developing a clear understanding of the organisation in which we work we are able to identify both potential problems or 'stressors' and sources of support. A greater level of awareness should enable us to have a greater say in what happens by preventing anticipated problems; controlling or influencing the types and levels of pressures experienced; developing strategies for coping; and maximising the availability and use of support systems. To work in an organisation without having a fairly clear understanding of how it operates, what its characteristics are and what hazards it presents is to take an unnecessary risk (or set of risks) as far as pressure and stress are concerned.

BEING 'STRESS AWARE'

If we combine self-awareness with organisational awareness, we have a good basis for developing stress awareness. By being 'stress aware' we can be better equipped to keep our pressures within manageable limits. As we have seen, stress is not something that affects only 'weak' or 'inadequate' people. Anyone can experience stress if the circumstances conspire against them at any particular time – we all have to avoid complacency by making sure that we do not assume that we are somehow invulnerable to stress, that it is just something that 'happens to other people'. The more tuned in we are to the three dimensions (stressors, coping methods and support) and how they interact with one another, the more equipped we will be to keep our pressures within manageable limits and keep stress at bay.

Being stress aware is also important in supporting others against stress – whether as direct colleagues or as managers, supervisors or mentors. It involves being able to recognise, not only in ourselves, but also in others, when pressures are reaching (or have crossed) the boundary between manageable, acceptable and safe on the one hand and unmanageable, unacceptable and unsafe on the other.

BOUNDARIES OF RESPONSIBILITY

A further important means of preventing stress is to recognise – and respect – the boundaries of responsibility (see Figure 6.2). Responsibilities can be divided into three distinct (but overlapping) categories:

Figure 6.2 *Boundaries of responsibility (based on training materials produced by Tony Morrison)*

I This refers to personal, individual responsibilities. There are many things that each of us is personally responsible for (for example, getting out of bed and getting ourselves to work on time).

WE There are other responsibilities that are shared. No single individual carries total responsibility, but each one has a degree of shared responsibility. Teamwork is a good example of a WE responsibility.

THEY This refers to matters for which we are not responsible, even though they may affect us very closely and very significantly. Corporate budgets or policies would be good examples for the majority of staff in most organisations.

The benefit of this framework as a stress avoidance tool is that it should help us to make sure that:

- we carry out our responsibilities at a personal (I) and collective (WE) level so that we do not face the additional pressure of the 'flack' that comes from other people when we shirk our responsibilities;
- we do not take responsibility for THEY matters, thereby giving ourselves unnecessary burdens to contend with. For example, if an organisational policy is not working effectively, this is likely to cause us enough problems without the additional onus of feeling responsible for, or guilty about, the shortcomings of a policy we did not create.

It is important to note, though, that these categories are interconnected. *My* responsibilities feed into *our* responsibilities, and (as in the example given above) WE have a responsibility to inform THEM that the policy is not working.

'Policing' the boundaries of responsibility can be a major way of fending off stress and should therefore be taken very seriously.

CONCLUSION

It is not always possible to avoid stress. There can be times when the pressures are too great and the level of support we need is not there. However, as this chapter has shown, there are various things we can do to minimise the chances of our pressures crossing that all-important line and becoming harmful stress. Underpinning all of these is the need to be *stress aware*, to be tuned in to the constant potential for stress (for ourselves, our colleagues and for friends and family too). Complacency about the significant risk involved is an unwise path to follow.

🔒 **KEY POINT**

The predominance of two-dimensional thinking means that some people are experiencing stress, but are reluctant to say so and get support, because they see it as amounting to admitting that they are weak or inadequate, while others are risking becoming stressed because they are complacently assuming that they are invulnerable.

EXERCISE 6

- What steps can you take to make sure that you remain stress aware?
- Who can help and support you in this?
- How can you help others to make sure that they become and remain stress aware?

Responding to stress

Preventing or avoiding stress is one thing, but what can we, or should we, do when things have gone beyond that, when we have actually got to the point where stress is being experienced? That is precisely the question that this chapter is geared towards answering.

RECOGNISING THE PROBLEM

The first point to emphasise is the importance of being both brave and sensible enough to acknowledge that there is a problem. Even in this day and age, when the pressures of modern working life are widely recognised, there is still a lot of stigma attached to being seen to suffer from stress (because of the pathologising tendencies of the two-dimensional model). It is not surprising, then, that many people are reluctant to accept that they are under stress, that the pressures they face are doing them harm in some way. Until it has been acknowledged that there is a problem, it is assumed that there is little or nothing to do. This has implications for three sets of people: (1) the employee concerned; (2) the line manager; (3) significant others.

The employee concerned

If I am not aware of what is happening to me, I will be in a very weak position to do anything about it. Unfortunately, it is not uncommon for people to 'slide' gradually into stress, without realising what is happening (there is a strong parallel with what often happens when people become depressed).

The line manager

There are two aspects to this. First, the line manager has to be able to recognise that one or more members of their staff are experiencing stress. Second, it is important that the line manager has the courage, confidence, sensitivity and skills to raise the matter with an employee who is not aware of the 'stress signals' they are giving off.

Significant others

This refers to people who play an important part in the employee's life, such as colleagues, relatives and friends. They too can at times recognise that someone is under stress, and they may or may not feel able to raise the subject with them. Ideally, all three sets of people identified here – the employee concerned, the line manager and significant others – will be able to work together to deal with the problems. For present purposes, however, we are going to concentrate on the role of the line manager or supervisor.

SUPERVISION

The term 'supervision' is generally used in two separate but related ways in a work context. It has a broad sense in which it refers to the general process of having oversight of an employee's work as part of the organisation's reporting structures and quality assurance system. In its narrower sense it refers more specifically to 'supervision sessions', one-to-one meetings between employee and line manager to discuss issues relating to workload, performance, training and development, and employee wellness. In terms of responding to stress, both senses of the term are very relevant.

Supervisory oversight

The line manager does not need to keep a close eye on everything an employee is doing, but he or she does need to have a reasonably clear picture of what is happening – level and nature of workload, capabilities and limitations and so on. Without this picture the line manager will not be in a good position to monitor levels of pressure and how the employee is responding to them. It will be difficult to respond to stress without this process of monitoring – without the right amount of supervisory oversight. Too much close supervision will run the risk of creating resentment in the employee and a feeling of not being trusted, while a lack of supervisory oversight will leave the line manager in a weak position when it comes to responding to the employee's stress.

Supervision sessions

Many organisations have a policy of regular, structured supervision sessions between worker and line manager (often as part of a broader process of appraisal or performance management). Where such policies exist (and are properly used), supervision sessions can provide excellent opportunities for not only recognising stress-related problems, but also responding to them by:

- helping the employee put their situation in perspective, recognising both problems and strengths to draw upon;
- exploring potential solutions or ways forward;
- identifying, and connecting with, sources of support; and
- offering reassurance and making it clear that the line manager is there to help.

Making supervision sessions work well involves a number of skills, but these are skills that are well worth developing to the full.

RECOGNISING STRESS

Stress is not an illness, and so it would be misleading to talk in terms of recognising 'symptoms'. None the less, there are signs and signals that can be detected when someone is under stress. These can be categorised under three headings: thoughts, feelings and actions (see Thompson, 2021, for a discussion of the THINK–FEEL–DO framework).

Thoughts

Under stress, people will often think less clearly or effectively, and memory may also be adversely affected.

Feelings

Anxiety and depression are both quite common reactions to stress. Feelings of confusion and disorientation are also not uncommon.

Actions

Our behaviour can change quite markedly as a result of stress, often leading people to see our actions as 'out of character'.

An important theme that runs across all three of these sets of signs is a deviation from normal patterns. For example, someone who is normally quite extrovert – the 'life and soul of the party' – may become quite withdrawn and introvert as a result of stress. By contrast, someone who is normally fairly quiet may become quite agitated or even manic. The trick, then, is to be able to recognise when someone is thinking, feeling or behaving in ways that are different from their usual ways of operating.

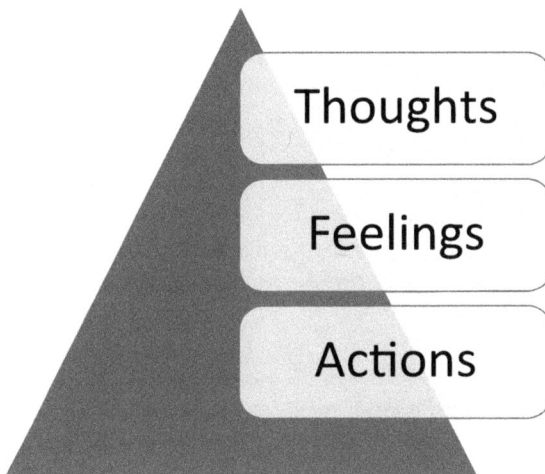

Figure 7.1 *Thoughts–Feelings–Actions*

Of course, there may be other reasons that explain these differences – they do not automatically mean that the person concerned is under stress (which is partly why it is important not to think in terms of 'symptoms' of an 'illness').

Conversely, someone may be under extreme stress, but manage to maintain their normal patterns – keeping the effects of stress well hidden beneath the surface. Stress, it must be emphasised, is a complex matter.

> ## 🔒 KEY POINT
>
> There will often be indicators that someone is stressed, but not always. We therefore need to: (1) be aware of what the likely indicators are; and (2) not make the mistake of being complacent by assuming that the absence of indicators can be equated with an absence of stress. We need to remain stress aware.

In addition to the three sets of signs outlined above, stress can also often be recognised as a result of the effects it has on the body. Although, stress is not an illness in its own right, it can:

- make us feel ill, with headaches, stomach aches and so on;
- exacerbate existing illnesses, such as asthma, psoriasis or heart disease; and
- lead to illnesses – for example, ulcerative colitis.

We return to the important topic of recognising stress in Chapter 13.

TAKING REMEDIAL ACTION

Once it has been recognised and accepted that stress is an issue that needs to be addressed, the next step is to decide what needs to be done to remedy the situation.

Circumstances will vary enormously, and so it is not possible for us to offer across-the-board solutions (nor would it be wise for us to try to do so). However, the following pointers should be helpful in many of the situations you are likely to encounter.

Start firefighting

Is there anything that needs to be done urgently to prevent the situation getting worse or to salvage important elements of it? Make sure that you are getting your priorities right.

Set boundaries

Establish who is responsible for what, who has control over what. This is not to allocate blame, but rather to clarify where the problems begin and end – so that the problems do not seem overwhelming and too complex to handle. Clarify which aspects of the situation are confidential and which can be shared with colleagues.

Control workload

What steps can be taken to make sure the employee's workload is reasonable and manageable? This may involve reallocation of some tasks, on a temporary basis at least, but an important feature of this should be establishing clarity about priorities – working out which tasks can wait, in order to create some breathing space.

Keep the channels of communication open

Stressful situations can be quite volatile and therefore prone to changing quite rapidly. It is therefore essential to monitor the situation closely and ensure that the relevant parties communicate effectively. It is ironic (and often tragic) that stressful situations underline the need for effective communication while the fraught nature of such situations often stands in the way of the right connections being made.

Identify and implement support systems

Clarify with the person concerned what supportive measures (drawing on both formal and informal support systems) can be pressed into action and decide which of these are likely to be appropriate and helpful. Steps can then be taken to mobilise the best combination of support opportunities.

Keep appropriate records

A subsequent inquiry or investigation into the factors leading to the present situation is possible. An accurate and appropriate record of the circumstances, the steps taken and the reasons for taking them may prove invaluable. Even without such an investigation, it is none the less good management practice to keep records so that the situation can be reviewed and lessons can be learned.

Avoid creating dependency

At the height of a highly stressful episode, it is understandable that it may be necessary to do certain things for the person concerned. However, we should be wary of overdoing this or doing it over an extended period of time, as this can lead to a form of dependency. It is therefore important that we should work towards empowering the individual to overcome their problems, rather than slot into too paternalistic a role.

Get support for yourself

Helping one or more people who are under stress can be a very demanding task. It can take its toll if support is not also available for those providing support to others. It is therefore important not to get so wrapped up in the situation as to lose sight of your own support needs. In particular, it can be important to have someone to 'bounce ideas off' – to reassure you that you are doing the right thing or to warn you of any actual or potential mistakes.

This is, of course, not an exhaustive list, but it should provide sufficient insight into the range of issues that is likely to be faced so that the task of 'taking remedial action' can be considered carefully.

CONCLUSION

Responding to stress issues when they arise is challenging, and there is no guarantee of complete success. However, as we have seen, there are steps that can be taken to make the response as positive and effective as possible.

The more positive and effective the response, the less negative the impact will be in terms of the significance of the aftermath of any such stressful incidents or ongoing situations. Once a period of stress is over, things will not necessarily return to normal straight away – indeed, the aftermath of a stressful situation can be felt for quite a considerable period of time. Because of this, Chapter 8 addresses what is involved in handling the aftermath in ways that minimise any further harm and significantly reduce the chances of a return to a stressful situation.

EXERCISE 7

- If you were going through a particularly stressful period in your life, how would you want the people around you (at work and at home) to respond?
- What would work best for you? What can you learn from considering these issues?

8 Dealing with the aftermath

Although there is, as we have seen in the previous two chapters, much that can be done to prevent stress from arising in the first place and to deal with it once it has arisen, what needs to be done to 'deal with the aftermath' has received far less attention and is consequently far less well developed. What we mean by 'dealing with the aftermath' is responding positively and supportively to someone who has experienced a very traumatic or extended period of stress, and is now attempting the sometimes very difficult transition back into 'normal' working life.

One of the great problems faced by someone who has been absent from work as a result of stress is that there is likely to be a fear that the same problems will recur, that history will repeat itself. The situation therefore has to be handled very carefully and sensitively in order to avoid returning to square one, particularly as such a result may actually begin another vicious circle in which the staff member's confidence is further undermined and their anxieties increased.

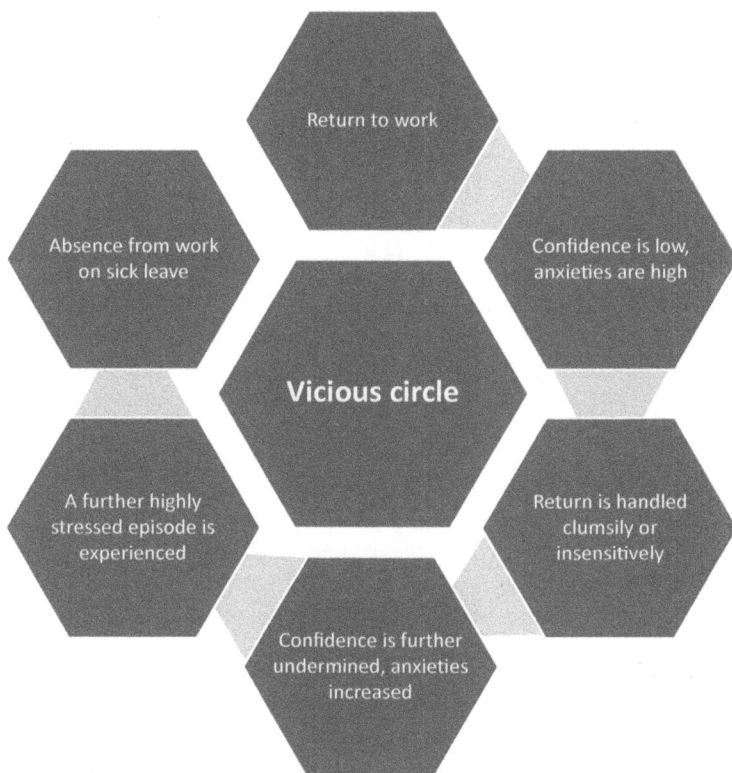

Figure 8.1 *The aftermath vicious circle*

Of course, where this leads to a further absence from work, any subsequent return is likely to be even more fraught, in effect 'upping the stakes'. Such a vicious circle can therefore easily contribute to the tragic discontinuation of a career. That is, the second return may be so traumatic that the staff member very quickly becomes absent again. This can then make the third return an enormous mountain to climb and may, in effect, lead to the member of staff never returning to their post, effectively abandoning their career.

PRACTICE FOCUS 8.1

Len was attacked by a member of the public in the course of his duties. Although not seriously injured, he was absent from work for almost a month as a result of a mixture of shock and stress – in effect, a form of post-traumatic stress. Len was very anxious about returning to work and was quite fraught on the day he did return. This was not helped by two key factors:

1. He faced a huge backlog of work – no one had covered for him during his absence.
2. While some colleagues were very supportive, others were quite insensitive and made jokes about the incident.

Len lasted only four days before going off sick again. Just over a week later he attempted to return again, but this time lasted only until lunch time. He went home in tears and, six weeks later, he tendered his resignation.

PREPARATION FOR THE RETURN

There are a number of steps that can be taken prior to the staff member's return to help facilitate a successful reintegration into the work environment. Many organisations have a sickness absence management policy which may provide guidelines on how the matter should be dealt with. For example, there may be stipulations concerning visiting or keeping in contact with the person concerned during the period of absence in order to:

- monitor the situation and note any progress or setbacks;
- offer appropriate assistance where possible;
- maintain official (and psychological) links between the employing organisation and the employee; and
- discuss and plan their reintegration, identifying any potential obstacles or pitfalls.

The first step that managers or supervisors need to take, then, is to check whether their organisation has such a policy and, if so, what obligations or expectations it brings to bear. In order to ensure the return to work is as painless and trouble free as possible in the circumstances, there are certain questions that have to be tackled. These include the following.

Which aspects of the situation are confidential and which can safely be shared with colleagues?

It is important to be clear about this so that confidentiality is not breached, but also so that information that may help colleagues facilitate the return is shared where this is appropriate. It will, of course, be necessary to consult with the member of staff concerned to establish their views about what information may or may not be shared. It is also advisable, in the interests of all parties, that such decisions are recorded to avoid any misunderstandings later.

Has the original problem gone away now or is it still there to be faced?

The answer to this question will have a crucial bearing on how the return should be handled. For example, if the main precipitating factor was work overload, have arrangements been made to ensure a fairer and more manageable workload? If, by contrast, the main stress factor was something that cannot be removed (a particular essential task, perhaps), then consideration should be given to how (1) the effects of this inevitable stressor can be cushioned; (2) the staff member's coping methods can be bolstered; and (3) he or she can be supported through the difficulties.

🔴 TIP

Try to think of support holistically, rather than just being a matter of making supportive noises. Reassurance is important, but so too are practical and emotional support. The broader our perspective on support the better.

Does the staff member have a balanced view of what led to the stress-related absence?

'Unbalanced' views can take different forms but the two most common are:

1. *Self-blame*: A common tendency among people experiencing stress is to be hard on themselves. One consequence of this may be that too much emphasis is placed on the individual's own part in the situation without due consideration of the wider context. As we have seen, stress is a complex, multifaceted phenomenon.
2. *Defensiveness*: The opposite scenario to self-blame is one in which a defensive response results in an unwillingness to look at one's own contribution to the situation in preference to blaming others entirely for what has happened.

What precise feelings is the member of staff experiencing?

While it should be crystal clear that the return has to be handled sensitively as far as emotions are concerned, we also need to be more precise about what feelings are involved. For example, fear and depression may require very different responses. Guilt may also feature (even where they have nothing to feel guilty about) or anger and disappointment may be more to the fore. Another factor to consider is that the situation may have triggered a grief response – the circumstances may have involved a number of losses that need to be grieved, not least a loss of pride, self-respect or confidence (Thompson, 2022).

Will they require some degree of workload relief?

Clearly it would be dangerous and unhelpful to throw someone in 'at the deep end' as soon as they return. Some thought will have to go into determining what is likely to be a reasonable workload: (1) during the initial resettlement period; and (2) on a longer-term basis thereafter.

Again, consultation with the member of staff concerned should prove invaluable in this regard. It should also be noted that giving someone too little work on their return may also prove to be problematic. This can have a deskilling effect and reinforce feelings of failure and inadequacy (see the Practice focus 8.2 below). The question of what constitutes an appropriate workload is therefore one that will need to be addressed and monitored.

What else needs to be done?

All situations are unique in some respects. It will therefore be necessary to look closely at the particular set of circumstances in question and decide what specific issues need to be addressed and what specific steps need to be taken. This is a process of 'personalising' the situation to the needs of the particular individual, rather than simply trying to fit him or her into a pre-existing framework – something that may lead to feelings of not being valued or recognised as a unique individual.

PRACTICE FOCUS 8.2

Siobhan found her work very demanding and struggled to cope with many aspects of it. After a year of struggling like this, she reached the 'last straw' and was away from work for over a month as a result of an accumulation of stress. When she returned to work, her line manager and colleagues were very sensitive and supportive. However, in some ways they turned out to be overprotective. In particular, Siobhan found herself on 'light duties', something she found helpful at first, but which later proved to be detrimental. The fact that her line manager continued to allocate only simple and straightforward tasks to her reinforced her feelings of inadequacy and her guilt at 'letting the side down'. An extended period of 'light duties' therefore seriously undermined her confidence — something which was fairly shaky to begin with.

Clearly, there are many important questions that have to be addressed if a successful reintegration into the work environment is to be facilitated. It may appear a daunting and demanding task, but it should be quite apparent that an investment of time, thought and energy into 'dealing with the aftermath' is a very worthwhile investment indeed.

CONCLUSION

A return to work after a period of stress-related absence can be a difficult process for all concerned – the member of staff involved, their colleagues and the line manager. Each has a part to play in contributing to the success or otherwise of the process of reintegration. Although we have focused in this chapter on the role of the line manager, perhaps the single most important person in all this is the individual member of staff concerned. It is they who perhaps face the biggest challenge. The points raised in this chapter should be of some help in meeting this challenge, but other chapters in this manual should also be of help in preparing for the demands of returning to a situation where stress was a major problem and may well become one again in the future. The 'aftermath' is therefore a challenging time for all concerned and needs to be considered very carefully, sensitively and thoroughly by everyone involved. It is to be hoped that this chapter can help to stimulate and guide such considerations.

EXERCISE 8

- In terms of dealing with the aftermath, what would you see as the three most important points to bear in mind?
- What makes them so important?

Avoiding burnout

As far as stress is concerned, 'burnout' is both a problem and a solution. It is a problem relating to stress in the sense that it can be seen as the result of exposure to stress over an extended period of time. It is also, in part at least, a solution to the problem of stress (or attempted solution), in so far as it blunts the emotions so that the pain of stress is felt less acutely. Burnout is a complex phenomenon and therefore one that needs to be looked at closely so that we do not fail to recognise or appreciate its insidious effects. It is a psychological condition characterised by three main features (based on the classic work of Maslach and Jackson, 1981):

- emotional exhaustion;
- lack of individual achievement; and
- depersonalisation.

These are very important issues and are worth exploring in more depth.

FEATURES OF BURNOUT

Emotional exhaustion

It is in this sense that burnout can be understood as an attempted solution to the problem of stress. This is because burnout involves getting to the point where our emotions are so overloaded that we become emotionally 'numb', as if we have somehow 'switched off' our feelings in order to protect ourselves from any further hurt or confusion.

Of course, as an attempted solution to stress, burnout causes more problems than it solves, as we shall see below when we look at 'The effects of burnout'. As we noted in Chapter 4, some coping strategies are ineffective and may even make the situation worse. To say that burnout is a form of solution is not therefore to put it in a positive light or to play down the harm it causes.

Lack of individual achievement

People who are experiencing burnout tend to 'go through the motions' of their work without necessarily achieving anything. For example, an administrative worker may be involved in processing a lot of paperwork but may do so in a very unproductive way, as if he or she is simply pushing pieces of paper around, rather than following a systematic work pattern that actually produces results.

This can be linked to the notion of 'routinisation'. Routines are, of course, an inevitable part of working life. It would be difficult, if not impossible, for any organisation to function without having a set of routines to rely on. However, there is a limit to the usefulness of routines, particularly for someone experiencing burnout who may try to do everything in a routine way, as if functioning on 'automatic pilot'. When this occurs, a further vicious circle begins – routinisation leads to a lack of stimulation and job satisfaction which, in turn, makes 'automatic pilot' and further routinisation much more likely to continue.

Depersonalisation

This refers to the tendency to treat people as if they were things, taking little or no account of their individuality, personal needs, characteristics and circumstances. This tendency can be apparent in medical settings where, for example, someone in hospital for an appendectomy is referred to as an (or the) appendix, as if all that exists is the problem, with no person attached to it!

Depersonalisation can feature quite heavily as a result of burnout. This can be linked to the emotional 'shutdown' mentioned above, where a member of staff cannot or will not accept the human dimension of the situations being dealt with – the feelings element is pushed to one side as far as possible. Depersonalisation involves a similar process – stripping the task down to its basic elements without addressing the 'people' aspects involved. It is as if the person experiencing burnout is trying to avoid or deny the human side of their work, as if it is too painful to face up to.

Burnout, then, can be recognised when we see someone who is emotionally exhausted or numb, relies heavily on routines or 'automatic pilot' and has a tendency to 'depersonalise' people. This paints a picture of a mechanistic approach to work, with little or no job satisfaction.

THE EFFECTS OF BURNOUT

It should be apparent from the above that burnout is a problematic condition for all concerned – the member of staff, their colleagues and line manager, possibly family and friends but almost certainly clients, customers or others who rely on a good service. Its negative effects include the following:

Low morale

The low or non-existent level of job satisfaction inherent in burnout is, of course, bound to contribute to a low level of morale, not only for the individual concerned, but possibly also for others around him or her. It is surprising how easily one burnt-out worker can 'spoil the atmosphere' and demoralise others. It is almost as if low morale were infectious. Low morale can easily become part of the culture and therefore a very powerful (negative) influence.

Low standards of work

There is a very high risk, in cases of burnout, that standards of work will be unacceptably low and that mistakes and misunderstandings will be unnecessarily high. In particular, there is an increased likelihood that important points or issues will be missed, that sensitive matters will be avoided or not even noticed. This can be especially problematic in work situations which involve some degree of sensitivity or heightened awareness.

Strained relationships

It can be very difficult to communicate or form a relationship where burnout is to the fore. Burnout can therefore be seen as a barrier to effective teamwork, and indeed can place a great strain on working relationships all around. In addition, these problems can cross the home/work boundary and result in strained relationships outside work too.

These are not the only detrimental effects of burnout, but should provide a sufficient insight into just how much of a serious problem of work psychology it can be. As a response to stress, it is clearly a very dangerous and harmful form of coping. Chapter 4 on coping methods should therefore be used as a means of exploring more helpful strategies for dealing with stress as part of an 'antidote' to burnout.

PRACTICE FOCUS 9.1

Ravi had worked in the customer service department for almost two years when a combination of pressures at work and the breakdown of his marriage plunged him into a state of burnout. He began doing his job mechanistically, with no real feeling or commitment for what he was doing. People were very unhappy with this – both customers and colleagues – but, as no one made a formal complaint, it became clear that the situation was likely to continue for a long time to come.

The condition of burnout can be a very difficult one to resolve, and its resolution may take an extended period of time while the situation is explored in depth and a range of possible solutions tried. Alternatively, some organisations may choose to deal with the situation within a much shorter time frame by seeking a solution through disciplinary or capability procedures – but even these can be very lengthy processes at times. It is therefore far preferable, where possible, to avoid the development of burnout in the first place. It is to some possible strategies for doing so that we now turn.

>>> REFLECTIVE MOMENT <<<

We will all feel tired, worn down and a little bit detached from our work at times, a long way from being on top form. But we should not confuse that with burnout, which is a much more serious problem and one that tends to apply across the board and throughout our working day – it is more than just a 'bad patch' or an off day. However, if you do feel that you are burnt out or that there is a very real danger that you will become so, then it is essential that you do something about it. An important first step is to identify the person(s) best placed to support you.

STRATEGIES FOR PREVENTING BURNOUT

Space does not permit an exhaustive account of preventative strategies, but what follows is intended as a guide to the types of approaches that can be used to reduce the chances of burnout becoming a problem for one or more staff.

Clarify and seek areas of job satisfaction

Work makes demands on all of us, but it also brings its rewards. Part of the fight against burnout is therefore a balancing act, making sure, as far as possible, that the rewards are not forgotten, or submerged under a sea of pressures and demands.

Some rewards or satisfactions are 'extrinsic' – that is, they are not part and parcel of the work itself: salary, 'perks' and so on. However, we should not neglect the intrinsic rewards – those satisfactions that are part of the job itself (working with people, perhaps, or completing certain tasks). Both types of reward, extrinsic and intrinsic, have an important part to play in maintaining a sense of job satisfaction.

Systematic practice

This refers to an approach to work that involves keeping a clear focus on what you are doing and why you are doing it (see Thompson, 2021). This can be achieved by using the following three questions as a guide:

- What are you trying to achieve? (your goals, objectives or desired outcomes)
- How are you going to achieve it? (your method, tactics or strategy)
- How will you know when you have achieved it? (indicators of success).

Such a systematic approach provides a degree of structure and focus that helps to avoid vagueness and drift. This helps to sustain levels of motivation and commitment.

Reflective practice

There are two basic aspects to reflective practice: reflection-in-action and reflection-on-action (Schön, 1983). The former refers to 'thinking on your feet', being alert to, and aware of, what is going on while you carry out your duties. This can be a demanding task that needs a lot of practice, but it represents a worthwhile investment of time and effort in preventing yourself from slipping into a rut of routines and mechanical processes. The latter refers to reflecting on our actions after the event so that we can learn from them – to rectify any problems that are identified and to build on strengths. One aspect Schön did not focus on was 'reflection-for-action' which refers to planning – that is, thinking ahead to be better prepared for what is to come. This includes anticipating difficulties (so that we are better placed to respond to them) and positive opportunities (so that we can capitalise on them).

Reflective practice can be very helpful in avoiding a reliance on unthinking routines that can lead to burnout.

Continuous professional development

Continuous professional development (or CPD, as it has come to be known) involves making a commitment to continuing to learn throughout one's career. This is not simply a matter of attending training courses, but rather, taking a much broader perspective on learning – recognising that the opportunities for learning and professional development are many and varied. A commitment to CPD can be a major factor in ensuring that burnout does not become a serious threat.

Work to live

While problems may arise as a result of a lack of commitment to one's work and the responsibilities associated with it, it can also become very problematic when we become overcommitted. That is, if we get into the habit of living to work (rather than working to live) we can lose the benefits, pleasures and supports that come from life outside work. Relying too heavily on the rewards of work itself can leave us vulnerable to burnout when those rewards become unavailable to us (as a result of stress, for example). It is therefore important that we maintain a balance between our lives within work and our lives outside work – to ensure that we are protected from the hazards of investing too heavily in our working lives at the expense of our private lives.

CONCLUSION

Burnout is a very serious and costly problem in the modern workplace. There are no guarantees that we can prevent it in all circumstances, but there is certainly much that can be done to reduce the chances to a minimum. In a sense, we have a double responsibility. First, we need to make sure that we are taking responsibility for our own health and safety (as the legislation requires us to do) by taking whatever reasonable steps we can to prevent burnout and to 'nip it in the bud' when it begins to feature. Second, it is also important that we play our part in supporting others to help them keep burnout at bay – or, where burnout has already arisen, doing whatever we reasonably can to be supportive in helping people escape its clutches.

EXERCISE 9

- If you were to become aware that you are in danger of burning out, what are the three most important steps you could take to fend it off?
- And what are the three most important things you could do to support a colleague who is burning out?

10   Becoming assertive

The first point we need to make here is that being assertive does not mean being stroppy, demanding, aggressive or nasty! Assertiveness is a word that is often misused and misunderstood. Basically, being assertive means finding the balance between not allowing yourself to be bullied and not bullying others. Indeed, this is what makes assertiveness very relevant to dealing with stress, as it involves exercising a degree of control and influence over our interactions with other people. This can give us opportunities to try and prevent other people's actions from causing us problems.

ESTABLISHING THE BALANCE

Interactions between people often involve a degree of tension and conflict, particularly where there is an underlying conflict of interest between the parties. Such conflict can lead to one person trying to dominate the other, or both persons trying to dominate each other.

This can produce a number of combinations as far as outcomes are concerned.

Aggressive-Submissive

This is where one party bullies the other into submission. This does not have to be 'aggressive' in the usual sense of being actually or potentially violent. Rather, it refers to the tendency to try and get what you want at the expense of the other person, without taking account of their needs, rights or interests. The person who is or becomes submissive gives up on their stake in the situation and concedes to the other party, even where this may have great personal cost at times.

Aggressive-Aggressive

This is a dangerous combination in which aggression is met by aggression, often leading to an escalation, which can produce a very unpleasant and unhelpful situation, and even to actual violence. This combination can be harmful and destructive not only at the time of the interactions, but also for weeks, months or even years after, as a result of the bad feelings generated. The situation may remain unresolved or may be resolved by one party backing down (thus producing an aggressive-submissive combination).

Submissive-Submissive

Perhaps the least common of the combinations, this one can easily result in stalemate (with nobody prepared to make a decision or move forward). In a submissive-submissive interaction, each party leaves it to the other to take a lead. This may be as a result of a lack of confidence, a fear of upsetting the other person, or some other anxiety. A common result is indecision and/or inaction, with neither party prepared to take responsibility for what is to happen or what needs to be done.

In each of these three cases, there is likely to be a much higher level of pressure than is necessary, thus increasing the likelihood of stress being experienced by one or more participants. In view of this, opportunities for avoiding these three combinations should be taken very seriously. This is where assertiveness comes in.

Assertiveness refers to the quality of being able to negotiate a constructive path between the two generally unhelpful extremes of aggression and submission. Developing this quality involves becoming quite skilled at handling interpersonal interactions.

I shall outline below some of the techniques that can be drawn upon as part of the process of developing those skills (see 'Steps towards assertiveness').

The aim of assertiveness is to create what are known as 'win–win' situations. This means working towards outcomes that are acceptable to both parties. This is not simply a matter of making compromises (as compromises often result in 'lose–lose' situations where neither party is satisfied but prefers to avoid further conflict). Rather, it involves looking calmly and carefully at the situation in order to try and find creative solutions that go beyond head-to-head conflict. The key to assertiveness is maintaining a balance: not getting what you want at the other person's expense, but not letting them get what they want at your expense.

PRACTICE FOCUS 10.1

Lyn was a training officer in a large company. She attended a meeting where she wanted to propose investing resources in a diversity training programme. However, there was clearly resistance to this idea from colleagues who did not wish to support her proposal. She was therefore under pressure to withdraw her proposal due to 'time constraints in the meeting'. Rather than simply backing down or risking alienating people by becoming aggressive, she argued that she should be given the opportunity to submit a written proposal to the next meeting of the group. She was delighted when this was accepted, as she felt that a written proposal would give her the opportunity to allay some of the anxieties that were probably contributing to the resistance she was encountering.

THE IMPORTANCE OF SAYING 'NO'

The greatest value of assertiveness as a stress management tool is probably that of saying 'no'. Indeed, being able to say 'no' to people or situations that will otherwise add significantly to the pressures you experience can be a major feature of a successful battle to keep stress at bay.

Often people will make unreasonable demands on us, and we may feel we cannot win. If we say 'yes', we end up with a task or responsibility that is going to prove very difficult and demanding. However, if we say 'no', we run the risk of upsetting or alienating the other person, possibly leading to further pressures for us. How can we get out of this without causing ourselves problems?

Partly it is a case of 'It's not what you say, it's the way that you say it'. Saying 'no' does not necessarily mean giving a flat refusal. There may be other ways round the situation, such as:

'I can't do that this week, but I may be able to fit it in next week, if that's not too late'.

'I could do half of that work but couldn't realistically manage it all. Is there anyone who could do the other half?'.

'I could do it, but I would have to postpone doing other important things to make room for it. How essential is it that I do this for you?'.

These are just some of the ways in which we can look for creative solutions between the two extremes of allowing ourselves to become overloaded and giving a flat refusal (although, at times, a flat refusal may well be the most appropriate response).

! TIP

If you find it difficult to say no in certain situations, think about the consequences of not doing so and then work out which is the lesser of the two evils. So often people will say yes when they should have said no and then regret having to suffer the consequences of doing so.

DEALING WITH YOUR FEELINGS

When we are faced with a situation where we need to be assertive, it is not uncommon to experience a 'fight or flight' response. That is, if we feel threatened, our body prepares itself either to engage in conflict (fight) or run away from it (flight). This means we will start to feel uncomfortable, tense and edgy. Being assertive involves trying to avoid both fight and flight by controlling our feelings to the extent where we are calm enough to deal with a difficult situation without 'fighting' (aggression) or resorting to 'flight' (submissiveness). As we shall see below, there are a number of techniques that can be drawn upon to help with this.

Although it is often difficult to control feelings, the benefits of doing so make it very worthwhile to devote time and effort to learning and practising the skills and methods that can prove so useful. Dealing with our feelings in this way can help to prevent negative and stressful situations later as a result of losing control over what is happening or how events affect us.

STEPS TOWARDS ASSERTIVENESS

A lot has been written about methods and techniques that can be used to develop assertiveness. Here, I shall limit myself to outlining a small selection of steps that can be taken towards assertiveness.

Honesty and openness

When we are open and honest about what we want and need, we are more likely to create a situation in which mutual respect will develop. It can therefore pay dividends to be clear about what we want and need, rather than simply drop hints or keep quiet and hope that the other person takes account of our position. Of course, this is not a technique that can be applied in any circumstances. Sometimes it is simply not safe to be so open and, in doing so, we may make ourselves prey to exploitation. We therefore have to be careful in choosing when it is safer to keep things to ourselves.

Gentle persistence

This refers to the process of continuing to ask for whatever we want or need, especially when we are being ignored or overlooked. It involves making our case clearly, firmly and calmly.

- *Clearly*: Leaving no room for doubt or ambiguity so that the other party cannot pretend they did not realise or appreciate what we wanted. The clearer we are, the less room there is for misunderstanding, but also the less room for anyone to distort the situation to try to exploit us if that is what they choose to do.
- *Firmly*: Being confident in making our claim so that we are not ignored, but without overstepping the mark and becoming aggressive. This can be about what we say (the actual phraseology we use), how we say it (our tone of voice) and whether our body language is reinforcing or undermining what we are saying.
- *Calmly*: Being gently persistent so that it becomes increasingly difficult for the other party to ignore us. It also avoids giving them an opportunity to be aggressive (which is what would happen if we were aggressively persistent). Again, this will involve not only what we say, but also how we say it.

The longer we are able to remain gently persistent, the stronger our case becomes and the more pressure we exert on the other party to be reasonable and listen to what we have to say.

Role play

Nervousness is a common obstacle to being assertive. If we feel nervous about speaking our minds or making our case, there is a danger that we will take the easy way out by not having the courage of our convictions, for example by not speaking up when we have the opportunity to do so. One way of dealing with this obstacle is to imagine that we are 'playing a role' when we do actually speak up for ourselves or do what is required of us in the interests of assertiveness. That is, we can create a bit of safe distance between ourselves and the situation we find threatening by imagining that we are not actually in it, that we are simply playing a role. This may sound a strange thing to do but it can be very effective by giving us just that little bit of safety and reassurance we need to deal with a difficult situation.

Breaking out of tramlines

Sometimes we may find it difficult to be assertive, because we get carried along by habit. We become trapped in the tramlines of responding to situations according to convention and habit, rather than according to what would be the best or most helpful way to respond. Often, for example, we may deal with a request in a non-assertive way simply because that is the way we are used to dealing with such requests, even though we may accept that this is not a helpful thing to do. One way of breaking out of such habits or sets of tramlines is to try and anticipate when they may arise – forewarned is forearmed. If we know in advance when a particular unhelpful response is likely to be triggered by habit, we can try to be ready for it and 'head it off at the pass' by taking action to break the pattern of slipping into a habitual response.

CONCLUSION

Being assertive involves using a set of skills, and so it can take time to become fully assertive if you have not already learned these skills. However, the process of skill development will not happen if we are not committed to being more assertive, and so the first step needs to be recognising how much we (and possibly people who rely on us) can be missing out on by not being sufficiently assertive.

As we have seen, there are tactics we can use and, with practice, we can all improve our assertiveness skills. We stand to benefit significantly, especially if, as is often the case, not being assertive enough is leading to stress.

🔒 KEY POINT

It is worth reinforcing the point that being assertive does not mean being pushy or difficult or throwing your weight about. It means having the skills, the patience and the presence of mind to negotiate win–win outcomes as far as possible – that is, to try and find ways forward that are positive for all involved.

EXERCISE 10

Think of somebody you know who you regard as being very skilled in assertiveness. Look closely at their behaviour, the body language they use, how they speak and so on.

- What is it that they are doing that makes them so successful at being assertive?
- What can you learn from this?

11 Handling conflict

However hard we work towards developing harmonious relations in our personal and working lives, it is of course inevitable that we will experience a degree of conflict from time to time. Indeed, for some people in some settings, conflict is part of the daily round, a common ingredient of life. Assertiveness, as discussed in Chapter 10, can and often does play an important role in handling such conflict. Indeed, the techniques discussed in that chapter can be pressed into service very well in both preventing conflict situations from arising and dealing with them once they do. However, there are also other factors above and beyond assertiveness that are very significant in relation to handling conflict. It is some of these factors that we are concerned with in this chapter.

RECOGNISING NEEDS AND INTERESTS

An important distinction to draw is that between positional negotiation and principled negotiation. Positional negotiation refers to the type of interaction that can so easily result in stalemate – a deadlock that can prove frustrating and unproductive for both parties. This can arise because neither person is prepared to concede ground or make concessions without an equivalent or more in return. Principled negotiation, by contrast, involves identifying:

- areas of common ground;
- areas of conflict and disagreement; and
- the underlying needs and interests of both parties.

Such an analysis can then form the basis of a constructive process of negotiation or conflict resolution during which positive ways forward acceptable to both parties can be explored and developed. This presents opportunities for creative solutions and the avoidance of the problems of stalemate and entrenchment associated with positional negotiation.

Unfortunately, the positional approach to conflict resolution tends to be far more common than the principled approach. Indeed, it is very easy to slide into a positional approach – establishing our position or territory and then defending it. And, of course, the problems that arise from this bring with them additional pressures and therefore increase the chances of stress being experienced. The efforts involved in developing a principled approach are therefore worthwhile in terms of avoiding or preventing stress.

The steps that can be taken to develop such an approach include the following.

- *Establishing your own position clearly*: What do you need from this situation? What do you want from it?

- *Establishing the other party's position clearly*: What do they need from this situation? What do they want from it?
- *Thinking creatively*: What possibilities exist for moving forward that incorporate as many of the needs and wants as possible?

REASONS TO BE ANGRY

One significant factor that can stand in the way of the satisfactory resolution of a conflict of interest is the existence of one or more emotional barriers. Anger, whether overt or beneath the surface, is one common example of this. Such anger generally arises as a result of the frustration generated by the conflict situation and can easily escalate if it is met by anger on the part of other people involved (see the discussion of assertiveness in Chapter 10).

Defusing anger is therefore an important part of conflict management (which, in turn, is an important part of stress management). A fundamental principle of defusing anger to bear in mind is that people get angry for a reason. That is, if we wish to respond effectively and appropriately to someone's anger, we need to take account of the reason or reasons for that anger. Understanding why someone has become angry will be very helpful in:

- suggesting possible ways to defuse the situation;
- giving us clues as to how the person will behave (for example, in terms of who the anger will be directed at); and
- providing the basis for building a rapport – something that can be very significant in a tense situation.

However, it has to be recognised that it can be difficult to concentrate sufficiently calmly on why someone is expressing anger at the time you are feeling the force of that anger! None the less, where sufficient presence of mind can be found to do so, recognising the underlying reason for anger can prove invaluable.

>>> REFLECTIVE MOMENT <<<

Think about how you are likely to feel when encountering someone who is angry.

Are you likely to back off (and potentially make them even angrier)? Are you likely to become angry yourself (and risk a dangerous confrontation)? The better your understanding of your own response to someone else's anger, the better equipped you will be to respond productively and helpfully, rather than risk making a bad situation worse.

Similarly, acknowledging the other person's feelings can also be a useful strategy, as this can allow him or her to move on beyond the anger, rather than get stuck within it. However, while it can be valuable to acknowledge feelings, this is not the same as simply saying: 'I know how you feel'. Of course, you don't know how they feel, and trying to make out that you do can inflame the situation even further. How you experience anger may be very different from how he or she experiences it, so you cannot assume that it is safe to say it.

PRACTICE FOCUS 11.1

Marcus, a personnel officer, was asked to deal with a sensitive matter relating to a man who was constantly entering into conflict with others, getting very angry in the process. Marcus's task was to try and avoid the need for disciplinary proceedings. He set about this task by deciding that it would be important, if not essential, to try and establish the reasons for so much frustration and anger. This he managed to do fairly quickly and was surprised by how successful this tactic proved to be. He was pleased that his training in conflict resolution had stood him in good stead.

RECOGNISING WARNING SIGNS

Where anger is not defused, there is a danger that aggression and violence may result. It is therefore important to be able to recognise the warning signs that can 'tip us off' to a violent outburst. Preventing or responding to aggression and violence is a complex subject, worthy of closer study and training so, for present purposes, we shall restrict ourselves to identifying some of the main nonverbal cues or warning signs:

- *agitation, restlessness and making frequent movements*
- *threatening gestures, provocative behaviour*
- *holding the gaze – eyeball-to-eyeball confrontation*
- *invasion of 'personal space' – coming too close*
- *banging the table or other furniture*
- *clenched fists*
- *towering posture*
- *obvious facial muscle tension*
- *poking fingers or pushing*
- *unusual or inconsistent behaviour, e.g. the noisy person who becomes quiet and withdrawn.*

(More, 1997, p 30)

By being able to recognise warning signs such as these, we should be in a stronger position to sidestep or otherwise deal with the potential for violence. This can not only help to prevent stressful or traumatic incidents but can also enhance confidence and boost coping abilities.

PROTECTING YOURSELF

Becoming more alert to the warning signs of potential violence is clearly an important part of protecting yourself from assault and the trauma that so often goes with it (see

Chapter 8). However, there are also other steps that can reasonably be taken to make sure that you are as safe as possible from attack. Such measures include:

- avoiding situations where you are left alone with an aggressive or potentially violent person; of course, it is not always possible to do this, but, by being alert to the situation and the possible warning signs, we can make ourselves much safer in many situations;
- making sure people know where you are and what time you are due back, so that you can be offered support if you need it; this is particularly important if you work in the type of setting where conflict, aggression and possibly violence are not uncommon;
- not 'cornering' people (literally or metaphorically) so that they do not feel the need to lash out to get out of a situation where they feel threatened or vulnerable; this is perhaps one of the most important pieces of advice, as cornering someone, making them feel that they are trapped, is a very risky thing to do;
- removing yourself from a situation where necessary – recognising when you have to give up on whatever you were trying to achieve and concentrate on getting yourself into a safe place; persistence and determination are important and useful things, but at times they need to take a back seat to your own safety or the safety of others with you;
- assessing risk by looking carefully at a situation and the threats it poses before allowing yourself to become immersed in it – an especially important tactic for situations where alarm bells have previously been ringing or are beginning to ring now; this is another reason why reflective practice, as discussed above, is so important and valuable.

Perhaps the most important theme underpinning all this is that of awareness. If we have a tendency to operate on automatic pilot, without considering carefully the situations we face, then we run the risk of encountering difficult, threatening interactions which may:

- bring us face to face with aggression and violence, without being adequately prepared to deal with them;
- expose us to additional pressures (and therefore the possibility of stress) as a result of the strong emotions that are generally generated by such encounters.

Developing awareness of potential threat situations is therefore an important and worthwhile task to commit ourselves to. It is part of the process of being stress aware.

BULLYING AND HARASSMENT

It is unfortunately sometimes the case that conflict situations arise in organisations as a result of senior staff abusing their positions of power by indulging in bullying and/or harassment. Senior staff have a degree of legitimate authority as far as 'subordinate' staff are concerned. However, there are legal and moral limits to the exercise of authority, and it is certainly not the case that 'anything goes' as far as the use of such power is concerned. As a result of legislation, it is increasingly common for organisations to have policies geared towards preventing and/or responding to incidences of bullying or harassment, particularly where persistent offenders are concerned. It is therefore wise to check whether your employing organisation has such a policy and, if so, what it says and how it works.

However, where possible, it is advisable to deal with such matters by 'nipping them in the bud', rather than waiting for them to develop to the point where the implementation of formal procedures becomes necessary. This is because the use of such procedures can, in itself, prove stressful as a result of the feelings and tensions that can be generated.

Bullying and harassment are very serious issues and so it is important that they are not 'brushed under the carpet', as they can be seen to be major sources of pressure, and therefore potentially of stress.

CONCLUSION

Conflicts can be positive at times, in so far as they can lead to fresh perspectives being generated; they can enable people to better understand one another's perspectives (by working through the conflict) and they can help organisations to have a fuller understanding of the dynamics going on within that organisation (and be better placed to benefit from them). However, unresolved conflicts can do a great deal of harm and can be major factors when it comes to stress (especially when those conflicts escalate into situations involving aggression and possibly even violence).

It is therefore very important that we take conflict issues seriously. The more fully we understand them, the better equipped we will be to deal with them positively and thereby reduce the likelihood of stress.

EXERCISE 11

In responding to conflict situations, it is important to get the balance right – not to pretend they do not exist, nor to overreact to them. Think of a time when you have not got the balance right.

- What led to that and what were the consequences?
- What can you learn from this about managing conflict?

12 Time and workload management

One of the most commonly mentioned sources of stress is that of workload pressure – too much work to do and too little time to do it in. It is therefore important to look at the skills and methods involved in time and workload management so that we can consider how these can be used to reduce the likelihood of experiencing stress. This chapter explores some of the key aspects of the challenge of making the best use of the time and resources available.

UNDERSTANDING TIME MANAGEMENT

To begin with, it is essential to appreciate the importance of the four basic principles that form the basis of my 'Time and Workload Management' e-learning course.

Too much work is too much work

Some people have found time management courses to be counterproductive. This is because they came away feeling demoralised – as if they were being blamed for not being able to cope with the workloads they were facing. It has to be recognised that, no matter how skilled you are at time management, there is still a limit to how much work can be done within a given timeframe. The responsibility for avoiding a work overload situation is therefore a shared one: individual staff need to be as skilled as possible in making the best possible use of the time and other resources at their disposal, while managers need to ensure that staff are not subjected to excessive or unrealistic levels of work demand (see Chapter 14). This is an important point to note, as a tendency to ignore the wider managerial context can lead to a cynical and dismissive attitude towards time management skills and methods.

We need to manage energy and motivation as well as time

An important point to recognise is that how much we achieve within a given timescale depends on not only how well-organised we are, but also how motivated we are – how much energy we are prepared to devote to getting the task done. Managing a workload therefore involves managing energy and motivation as well as actual time.

Time and workload management involves skills, not qualities

It is sometimes thought that the ability to be well organised and keep a clear focus is a quality that some people have and some people do not. However, this is a defeatist view, as it does not recognise that what we are talking about is skill – skills that can be learned from training, coaching and experience. If you are not well organised now, you can learn how to become so, rather than have to accept that this is a quality you do not possess. Let us now look at each of these three principles in a little more detail.

Investing time to save time

Often it is necessary to make changes to how we work and making these changes (for example, putting new systems into place) can take time – time that many busy people will understandably claim that they do not have. However, this principle teaches us that it can be wise to invest time to save time – that is, the time and effort we put into making such changes will be repaid, with interest.

A MANAGEABLE WORKLOAD

I am not arguing that everyone should have an easy life and not have to worry about hard work or a range of different pressures. On the contrary, as noted earlier, too little pressure can in itself be a source of stress. My point, rather, is that a manageable workload may well be a very heavy workload indeed. What is important is not so much the amount, or even nature, of the workload, but rather whether the work demands are within the capacity of the individual, given their:

- experience, skills and training;
- access to tools, resources, systems, information and so on;
- support systems – depth, breadth and availability; and
- current level of functioning (which may be adversely affected by ill-health, bereavement or other such factors).

Where a workload exceeds an individual's capacity to deal with it, it becomes unmanageable.

Once this point is reached, a number of dangers appear.

- Mistakes become increasingly likely, perhaps very costly or even disastrous mistakes; this can then set off a vicious circle, in so far as the consequences of those mistakes can lead to additional pressures, potentially pushing us over the line from a manageable level of pressure to an unmanageable one.
- The quality of work is likely to suffer, perhaps leading to complaints or other problems that can bring additional pressures that also lead to a vicious circle developing; a reduction in quality of work can also lead to a loss of pride in our work, lower job satisfaction and thus negative consequences all round.
- Corners have to be cut to survive, and this can lead to important tasks not being completed. A common theme in formal investigations and inquiries into where things have

gone tragically wrong is that corners were cut, with disastrous consequences. Cutting corners is a very risky business indeed and, even if things do not go badly wrong, the extra pressure of knowing that they could can be sufficient to lead to stress.

- The focus of work can be lost, resulting in a lot of wasted time and effort and again a possible vicious circle. When people lose focus, things can drift, resulting in 'losing the plot' and thereby being largely ineffective. Clearly, this is not a sound basis for job satisfaction and a positive working environment.
- The loss of control involved in an unmanageable workload can be a major factor in turning pressure into stress. As we have noted, a sense of control is a key factor in keeping stress at bay.

This raises the question: How can we avoid (or get out of) a situation in which our workload is unmanageable? This is not an easy question to answer, but three pointers should be helpful. First, it is important to be realistic and recognise our limitations. If others have unrealistic expectations of us, we should be wary of taking this on board ourselves and seeing ourselves as inadequate or as failures. Second, it is important to be assertive (as discussed in Chapter 10) and bring our difficulties to the attention of others, particularly our line manager. For some people, it may seem risky to bring a work overload situation to a line manager's attention (in case this is seen as a sign of weakness), but this risk has to be balanced against the dangers outlined above of being unrealistic about an unmanageable workload. Third, the value of teamwork and a collective, collaborative approach should also not be forgotten.

🔒 KEY POINT

Organisational culture can be very significant. Some cultures encourage teamwork, collaborative approaches and mutual support – all valuable assets when it comes to time and workload management – while other cultures foster a very individualistic 'head down and get on with it' approach that can be very problematic. It can therefore be helpful to consider the culture you work in and explore whether you can influence it in a positive direction.

MANAGING TIME AND ENERGY

It is ironic that habits and routines which can be great time-saving devices, can also involve an enormous waste of time. The trick, of course, is to be able to recognise the difference between those situations where habits and routines tend to be helpful and those where a more thoughtful or creative approach is called for. To rely on habit where this is going to be ineffective is clearly a waste of both time and effort.

It is for this reason that much of the literature on time management concentrates on analysing the use of your time (for example, by keeping detailed time sheet records), so that you can identify the patterns of your time usage. This enables a more efficient use of time to be devised by identifying alternative ways of organising your time so that more can be achieved during the time available.

PRACTICE FOCUS 12.1

Margaret was constantly getting behind schedule with her work until she went on a time management course. Here she learned how to analyse her use of time and, from this, to identify which times were her most productive and which were her least. From this she was able to revise her work schedule and come up with new patterns of work that proved far better suited to the demands of her job.

While this 'time mechanics' approach clearly has benefits, we must also recognise its limitations. This can be seen to apply in two main senses.

1. The approach can easily become too mechanistic and can even be counterproductive when the time and effort expended are not compensated for by the efficiency gains achieved. This can also be a demotivating factor.
2. It does not take account of the far greater gains that can be achieved by concentrating on energy and motivation, rather than the minute details of time usage itself.

What, then, is involved in managing our own energy and motivation? This is again a complex question, but the following elements can be seen as at least part of the answer.

Get your timing right

Are you a morning person? Or do you function best in the afternoon or evening? Fitting the tasks you have to do into the time that suits you best can be a major help in terms of maintaining energy and motivation, if you are fortunate enough to have the flexibility to adjust your tasks and timing in this way. It can therefore pay dividends to look closely at the 'peaks and troughs' of your motivation levels and make the best use of them. For example, it would clearly be a mistake to attempt the most demanding of your tasks at the times when your level of energy is at its lowest.

Understand your job satisfaction

What is it about your job that you like? What are the rewards and satisfactions that keep you going? By understanding what it is about your work that you find satisfying and motivating, you can gain a clearer picture of which aspects you want to concentrate on so that you can maintain or enhance your levels of energy and commitment.

There is also much to be gained from simply being aware of – and appreciating – those aspects of your work that you find satisfying and rewarding.

Be clear about what you are doing and why

As noted in Chapter 9, motivation can be lost when we 'lose the plot', when we lose track of what we are doing and why we are doing it. Ironically, it seems that it is when we are under time pressures that we are more likely to slide into this unfocused 'drift' in which we have lost sight of what we are working towards.

The right person for the job?

There are tasks you might enjoy which a colleague may hate. Similarly, there may be aspects of your job that you do not like doing which someone else may be quite happy to do. There is therefore a lot of mileage in exploring the possibilities of sharing out particular tasks and duties with colleagues to ensure that you get the best person for the job – and thus help to sustain levels of motivation.

Of course, these are not the only ways of trying to keep energy levels up. Indeed, much of what was discussed in Chapter 9 in relation to avoiding burnout can also be seen to apply here in relation to maintaining motivation and commitment more generally. For example, the stimulation and motivation to be gained from continuous professional development are very relevant here.

DEVELOPING SKILLS

There are a number of techniques or 'tricks of the trade' that can be used to develop time management skills (see Thompson, 2021, Chapter 2). There are, therefore, materials to be drawn upon, but, as in matters of learning and development more generally, it is up to you to find what works for you and to adapt it to your purposes and the setting in which you work.

Another important aspect of skill development is the use of the CIA framework discussed in Chapter 6. This brings us back to the recurring theme of control: what aspects of our workload and our use of time are within our control? Which aspects can we influence, if not control? And which aspects can we neither control nor influence, and therefore have to accept?

By trying to answer these questions you should be able to get a clearer picture of the range of demands upon you and gain some idea of possible strategies for managing these demands as effectively as possible, seeking to make the best use of the time and other resources available to you. Of course, this approach requires a degree of confidence and self-awareness, but with experience, application and – where possible – support, these can be nurtured and developed as part of a process of continuous professional development.

INVESTING TIME TO SAVE TIME

This involves a form of reflective practice in which we need to take time to review how we are using our time and energy resources and trying to find ways of getting better results. This review can include setting priorities; identifying which of our activities take up more time or effort than is justified by the results produced; developing better systems for managing the masses of information the modern world throws at us; and so on.

It is basically a matter of avoiding the mistake of just pressing on with the pressures we face and assuming that, because we are busy, we do not have time to stop, think, plan or review the situation. That mistake can lead us into a hamster wheel situation in which we are putting in a great deal of effort but not getting very far because we have lost sight of the situation we are dealing with and are therefore less well equipped to deal with the challenges it presents.

CONCLUSION

These four principles will not tell you everything you need to know about time and workload management, but they should provide a sound foundation for you to build on as you develop your knowledge, skills and confidence in this area.

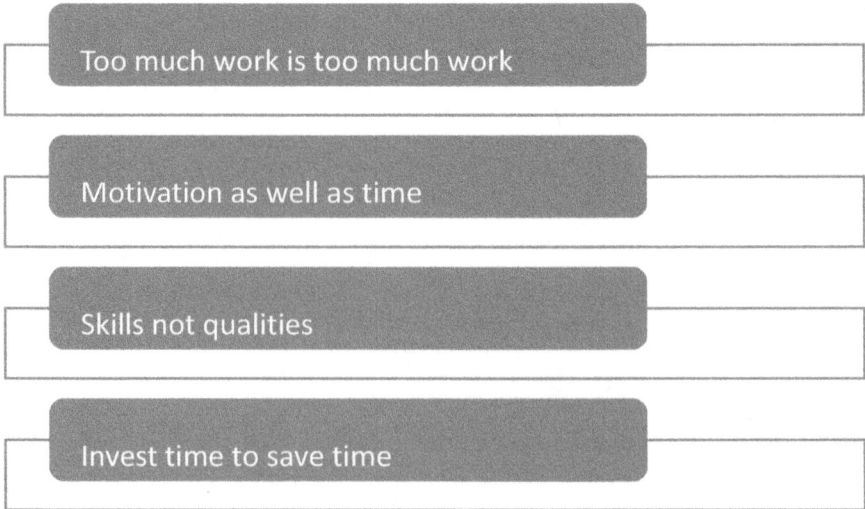

Too much work is too much work

Motivation as well as time

Skills not qualities

Invest time to save time

Figure 12.1 *The four principles of time and workload management*

EXERCISE 12

- Consider each of the four principles and identify at least one way per principle you feel you could improve your time and workload management. The more ways you can identify, the better.

13 Supporting each other

One of the most important aspects of dealing with stress is, as we saw in Chapter 5, support. While the focus in that chapter was on accepting, seeking and using support, this chapter looks at the situation from a different angle. It explores what is involved in offering support, creating the right sort of atmosphere in which support is an accepted part of the organisational culture.

What we need to consider, therefore, is what steps need to be taken to ensure as far as possible that a supportive environment really exists for staff. My view is that these steps are a shared responsibility. Although managers clearly and undeniably have a responsibility to manage the organisation (that is, after all, what they are paid for), everybody is a 'stakeholder' and therefore has an interest in creating and maintaining a supportive environment. This chapter, therefore, is not designed specifically for managers, but rather applies to all members of the workforce.

RECOGNISING STRESS

If we are going to be supportive of one another in fending off stress, it is important to be able to recognise when someone is showing signs of stress so that we can:

- 'nip it in the bud' by being supportive in the early stages before the problem has taken hold and started to do harm; this is again part of being stress aware by being tuned in to likely signs of stress and being prepared to offer appropriate support sooner or later. Having a supportive culture in the first place is also an important part of this;
- offer support in dealing with the situation on a 'remedial' basis – that is, recognising the damage that has been done, trying to remedy it and/or prevent it getting worse; what can easily happen when someone is stressed is that they withdraw into themselves (as a sort of protective measure) and, when this happens, it is not uncommon for others to 'back off', thereby leaving the stressed individual unsupported at the very time they need support the most;
- identify the sources of stress so that, where appropriate, steps can be taken to prevent other people from being affected by them. When we discussed coping earlier, I made the point that *active* coping based on problem solving is likely to be far more effective than simply trying to adjust to a bad situation. Consequently, working out what the sources of the stress were and trying to do something about them is a wise strategy.

But, how do we recognise stress? As we have noted, stress is not an illness, and so it is not a matter of identifying 'symptoms'. There are signs that can be very significant, but there are two important points we have to bear in mind in relation to these below.

- No individual sign is a sufficient indicator on its own – what we need to look for is a pattern or set of interconnected signs. It can be very misleading to focus on just one sign when there may well be reasons other than stress why that particular sign is being noticed (for example, someone may become withdrawn for a while, not because they are stressed, but because they are unwell or there is something on their mind that is distracting them or for various other reasons). It is therefore important that we do not jump to conclusions based on limited evidence. We have to look more closely than that and bear in mind *patterns* of signs.
- But we also have to bear in mind that signs are individualised – that is, your way of showing you are stressed may be very different from mine. We are not looking for standard patterns that apply across the board, regardless of the individual. Each of us reacts to pressures in our own way, and so the patterns we are looking for need to relate specifically to the individual concerned. This highlights the importance of identifying *changes* in behaviour. For example, if we notice that a colleague who is normally polite and courteous has become curt and abrupt, this may be telling us that stress is an issue, in which case we would need to consider whether there were other stress indicators present.

Common themes that can be identified are signs of tension, distress or discomfort. These can come in many shapes and sizes, but one useful way of categorising them is as follows:

- *health related* – aches and pains and/or a worsening of existing health problems, such as asthma, eczema or psoriasis;
- *cognitive* – difficulty in thinking clearly, problems with memory and so on;
- *emotional* – strong emotional responses such as anger, withdrawal, weepiness;
- *communicative* – communication difficulties or changes, whether verbally (for example, an unusual or inappropriate tone or style of language) or nonverbally (strong messages given by body language);
- *behavioural* – a wide range of possible behaviours that can give us clues that 'all is not as it should be'.

This is not a comprehensive or exhaustive list, but it should be enough to give a picture of the range of factors that we are dealing with when we try to become aware of the telltale signs of stress.

One final point worthy of emphasising again is that stress can often be indicated by *changes* in characteristic actions or attitudes. For example, a quiet person may become more vocal; an outgoing person may become withdrawn. Consequently, what we are often faced with, in trying to support colleagues, is the challenge of being able to identify differences between their current behaviour or approach and their more usual characteristic way of operating. That is, it is not simply the action itself that might give us clues, but also how and to what extent this differs from what we would normally expect.

It therefore pays to have at least a basic awareness of what constitutes 'normal' behaviour in our colleagues – otherwise, how will we be able to recognise significant changes?

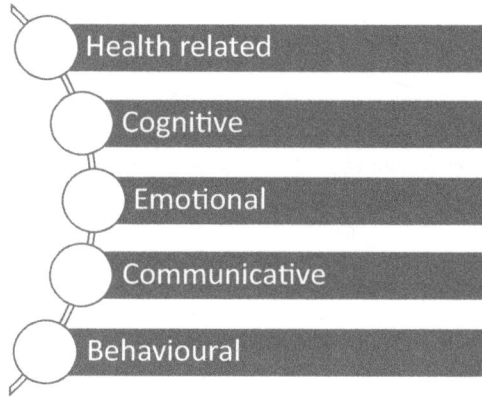

Figure 13.1 *Types of stress indicator*

WORKING TOGETHER

One common characteristic of people under stress is the tendency to go into their own little world, to concentrate on their own problems and concerns and perhaps isolate themselves to a certain extent from other people and networks. Where a team or staff group are under stress, this can create a 'separate worlds' problem. That is, despite the whole team collectively being under stress, there is no collective response or strategy, as each individual has gone into their own separate world, cut off from the wider picture and the possibilities of mutual support or a united effort to deal with the problems.

PRACTICE FOCUS 13.1

Siân was pleased to be appointed as team manager. However, she quickly realised that her staff team had been under immense pressure during their 'leaderless' period between her predecessor's departure and her arrival. She was disappointed to note that they had not supported each other during this time and had withdrawn into their own space, totally neglecting team issues. In effect, they had given up on being a team, a process reinforced by the self-isolating effects of stress. Siân therefore set herself the task of rebuilding a sense of teamwork and collective responsibility, and she sought advice from her own line manager about how best to go about this. Teamwork and a collective responsibility for tackling stress issues are clearly important elements of a strategy for developing a supportive work environment. But what is involved in good teamwork? What does it depend upon? The following pointers certainly do not constitute a comprehensive answer, but should provide a basis from which to develop an understanding of the complexities of teamwork and effective collaboration.

Communication

Keeping the channels of communication open (and trying to make sure that the necessary information is shared with the people who need to know it) is a basic ingredient of teamwork. Efforts should therefore be made to ensure that effective communication is a feature of the team's work. While managers have a responsibility for communication systems within an organisation, all staff share a responsibility for making such systems work.

Honesty and openness

Teamwork is hampered by hidden agendas, collusion and a basic lack of trust. It is therefore important to work towards openness where issues are dealt with constructively 'on the table', rather than secretively 'under the table'. Without this openness, conflicts (and all teams have conflicts) are likely to fester and become ingrained, rather than be tackled, dealt with and left behind. Of course, it has to be acknowledged that openness can sometimes appear dangerous in an atmosphere where there is little or no trust – see the discussion below of the 'ethos of permission'.

Clarity of purpose

While uniformity across a whole team is certainly not to be encouraged (not least because of its dampening effect on creativity), some degree of clarity of common purpose is essential. That is, if people are pulling in different directions, then the likely result will be unnecessary additional tensions and pressures, and a lack of teamwork and effective collaboration. Discussions focusing on developing a shared vision and sense of purpose therefore have an important part to play.

Affirming diversity

People come to teams with different backgrounds, experiences, skills, cultures and perspectives. While some traditionalists may see such diversity as a problem or a drawback, it can more usefully be seen as an asset – a basis for learning, breadth of vision and creativity. It is therefore important to affirm the value of a diverse workforce so that the strengths within the team can be recognised and built upon as part of a process of team development.

Change management

Teams change over time. A positive, effective, supportive team can lose its strengths over time, perhaps through complacency, through not adjusting to changes outside the team or as a result of changes in the team itself. Teams therefore need to be aware of the need to adapt to changes so that their strengths are not dissipated over time.

This includes 'succession planning'– making adjustments when members leave and effectively inducting new members so that they feel they belong and have a contribution to make.

Although good teamwork can be a very significant part of creating and maintaining a supportive environment, it should also be remembered that individuals may have specific support needs above and beyond what the team can offer. Teamwork is a major part of support, but it is of course not the only one.

AN ETHOS OF PERMISSION

The team 'ethos of permission' refers to a workplace atmosphere in which open expression of feelings is permitted and even encouraged. Some work settings have a very strong and well-established ethos of permission, while others have quite the opposite – a 'macho' environment in which certain sensitive topics are treated as taboo. Most work settings would appear to fall somewhere in between these two extremes.

An ethos of permission can be said to exist where it is acceptable within the organisational or team culture to:

- *admit mistakes* – to acknowledge how and where things have gone wrong so that these mistakes can be learned from and avoided in the future. Cultures where people are too anxious – or even afraid – to admit mistakes are not healthy places to work;
- *express feelings* – to be able to say openly 'I'm feeling worried'; 'I'm frightened by'; 'It's painful for me because' or other such emotive statements, without fear of being labelled 'soft' or 'weak'. Feeling hampered in being able to express emotion can contribute to the pressures we feel, while being able to 'ventilate' those feelings can be very positive and helpful;
- *talk about feelings generally* – to be able to discuss them openly as legitimate matters of concern, rather than suppressed at times when emotional issues are not to the fore. Having 'taboo' or 'no go' areas creates unnecessary tensions and hampers progress in dealing with issues that may be contributing to stress.

Once again it is the case that managers carry a responsibility for playing a lead role in creating and maintaining a healthy organisational climate and ethos. However, it remains the case that all staff or 'stakeholders' in the organisation have a part to play in this. Consequently, we can all make a contribution to creating or enhancing an ethos of permission.

🛈 TIP

Beware of the mistaken assumption that it is only managers who are responsible for the workplace culture and whether or not there is an ethos of permission. Every member of an organisation plays a part in shaping the culture. Don't disempower yourself by assuming you have no role to play.

This is not an easy undertaking, and it is likely to take a long time before its effects can be fully felt and firmly established. However, by supporting one another, by encouraging honesty and openness, and by recognising and affirming that stress is not simply a matter of weakness or personal inadequacy, we can begin to challenge and undermine the 'macho' assumptions that stand in the way of progress.

CONCLUSION

Supporting each other in managing the pressures we face is vitally important if we are serious about doing everything we reasonably can to keep stress at bay by keeping pressures within manageable limits. Some workplace settings are excellent examples of how effectively this can be done and what a positive impact supportive cultures can have. However, it is also sadly the case that very many workplaces have no such supportive culture, and the ethos is a macho, competitive and even hostile one.

In such circumstances we face two sets of challenges.

1. Doing everything we can to survive – and thrive, where possible – within such a context.
2. Making a contribution to try and change that culture, to work together to try and make it a more supportive working environment.

The more successful we are in rising to these challenges, the less likely it will be that stress will be a problem.

EXERCISE 13

- How would you rate your workplace in terms of supportiveness – low, medium or high?
- Are you able to identify ways in which you can improve this by addressing any problems and building on any strengths?
- Who would be your best allies in doing this?

14   Investing in the future

We have explored and examined a wide range of issues relating to stress, how it arises and what can be done about it. It should be clear from all this that stress is an extremely complex topic, and one that is not best tackled by some of the simplistic solutions that have commonly been taught and tried in the past. Indeed, it should be apparent that a more sophisticated, more carefully developed and thought-out approach is called for if we are not to run the risk of making matters worse by tinkering with an intricate and deep-rooted set of problems. The aim of this final chapter, then, is not to offer simple solutions, but rather to help clarify what is involved in developing a more realistic approach to tackling stress.

There is a well-known joke where someone who is lost asks directions, only to be told: 'I wouldn't start from here if I were you'. This is something that applies very much to stress – it is no good starting to think about how you deal with stress at the point where it is already doing a lot of harm. It is, of course, much better to plan ahead, to make sure you avoid the difficulties, rather than wait for them to arise and then think about tackling them. Forewarned is forearmed, and when it comes to being forewarned about stress, we have to be realistic and accept that no organisation is immune from stress – all organisations run the risk of being adversely affected by stress at some time or other. It therefore pays to have a strategy in place before problems arise or before they get out of hand. What is needed, then, is a workplace well-being strategy – a plan for dealing with stress matters in the workplace.

WHAT IS WORKPLACE WELL-BEING?

Workplace well-being is a relatively new idea in the management and organisational psychology literature, although now firmly established. It refers to an approach to human resources based on the principle that the effectiveness of an organisation depends to a large extent on its staff being adequately supported in carrying out their duties. The major implication of this approach is that organisations should invest time, effort and money in providing sufficient and appropriate support for their staff. But what is involved in providing such support? What investment has to be made in order to make the future as stress free as possible? These are the questions the remainder of this chapter seeks to address.

DEVELOPING A WORKPLACE WELL-BEING STRATEGY

An important first step towards promoting well-being is to identify the existing policies and practices that are geared towards supporting staff in some shape or form. These are likely to include:

- induction;
- training and development;
- supervision;
- appraisal;
- grievance procedures; and
- compassionate leave.

Less common, but increasingly being used, are confidential counselling schemes, whether run in-house or contracted out to a private agency.

Once this exercise has been completed, attention can then be focused on identifying what further steps are possible to safeguard the well-being of staff and help equip them to deal with the demands and challenges they face in their work.

The main benefit of thinking in this way about workplace well-being (identify existing policies; identify gaps) is that it provides a platform for developing a 'positive' approach which incorporates both existing strengths and actual or potential weaknesses.

A further benefit of identifying current support measures is that these can then be affirmed and consolidated. This can provide a positive beginning for a process that can lead to significant developments in workplace well-being. However, it also has to be recognised that it can be very difficult in some work settings to be at all positive due to the prevalence of a negative and defeatist organisational culture. Indeed, changing an organisation's culture can be a major feature of developing workplace well-being if such efforts are not to be tokenistic or superficial.

INFLUENCING THE ORGANISATION'S CULTURE

An organisation's culture – the unwritten rules and taken-for-granted assumptions that shape people's actions and interactions in the work context – can be influenced in a number of ways. This is, of course, linked to power. The more power an individual or group has, the more they can influence the way things work and the culture on which this is based.

But we can all influence culture up to a point, even if only by refusing to reinforce it through our own actions and attitudes. That is, we can all play at least a small part by helping to promote an approach to stress which:

- sees it as an organisational problem, rather than a sign of weakness or inadequacy in the individual;
- takes the problem seriously and actively adopts measures to prevent and counter it;

- recognises the legal implication of promoting workplace well-being as part of a framework of health and safety; and
- does not treat the problem as simply a fashionable topic of concern and therefore something to be dealt with tokenistically.

Each of these four points is very important in its own right and is therefore worthy of closer attention. We shall look at each of these in turn.

The organisational roots of stress

The point has already been made that stress should not be seen in narrow, individualistic terms, as the broader organisational context is a major factor in how stress arises, how it is experienced and how it is dealt with. An important element of workplace well-being, therefore, is to make this organisational focus clear and explicit in order to challenge the common tendency to conceive of stress as a matter of personal failing.

Some employers make the organisational focus clear by having policy statements and/or information leaflets which make explicit the shared responsibility of employer and employee for tackling stress, with comments such as:

> *Stress has a detrimental effect on the individual's health and also on the effectiveness of the company. The directors and managers are therefore committed to working with staff at all levels in the organisation in order to prevent stress as far as possible and to minimise its negative effects.*

But, of course, broad statements are of little value if they are not translated into practical reality on a day-to-day basis. An explicit acknowledgement of the organisational roots of stress is a good beginning – but it is only that, a beginning.

One step that can help make the broad commitment a concrete reality is a stress audit. This involves a survey to identify the stressors that staff face. From this, it can be established which of the stressors are the responsibility of the organisation; an action plan for tackling them can then be devised. For example, a common stressor identified by surveys is the physical working environment. Overcrowding, a lack of facilities or some other problem with the work environment can be an additional source of pressure that can, potentially at least, be addressed by the organisation itself if the political will is there.

A proactive approach

Over the years there has been a lot of research into occupational stress, and we have steadily developed a more in-depth understanding of some of the complexities. One message that has emerged quite clearly from this is that much stress is preventable. That is, there are a number of steps that can be taken to reduce the risk of stress being experienced.

- Are workloads manageable and properly monitored?
- Are staff appropriately briefed and trained for the duties they carry?
- Are staff adequately supervised and supported?

- Do they have the resources they need to carry out their work?
- Are their efforts appreciated and their contribution valued?

But, perhaps the most important and telling question of all is: If the answer to any of the above questions is 'no', does the organisation take responsibility for addressing the situation or is the hard-pressed employee left to shoulder the burden? A proactive approach is one in which this final question is taken seriously and properly addressed before the damage is done.

Health and safety

The legal position in relation to health and safety is well summarised in the following extract from the Health and Safety Executive guidelines:

> There is no specific legislation on controlling stress at work. Not enough is known to set detailed standards or requirements. However, employers have a duty under the Health and Safety at Work, etc., Act 1974 to ensure, so far as is reasonably practicable, that their workplaces are safe and healthy; under the Management of Health and Safety at Work Regulations 1992 employers are obliged to assess the nature and scale of risks to health in their workplace and base their control measures on it.
>
> Ill-health resulting from stress caused at work has to be treated the same as ill-health due to other physical causes present in the workplace. This means that employers do have a legal duty to take reasonable care to ensure that health is not placed at risk through excessive and sustained levels of stress arising from the way work is organised, the way people deal with each other at their work, or the day-to-day demands placed on their workforce.
>
> (Croner-i, 2024)

Clearly, then, there is a legal responsibility for employing organisations to safeguard their staff from undue hazards, including the very real hazards of stress. Indeed, the same guidelines go on to point out that:

> employers should bear stress in mind when assessing possible health hazards in their workplace, keeping an eye out for developing problems and being prepared to act if harm to health seems likely; in other words, stress should be treated like any other health hazard.

Beyond fashion

In recent years stress has become a major topic of concern and has, in some respects, become a 'fashionable' issue. While it is good to see the serious problem of stress being given a lot of attention, one very real danger is that the fashionable aspect of stress leads to it being treated superficially and tokenistically, with some organisations 'going through the motions'. It is therefore very important to be wary of tokenistic measures, such as:

- rhetorical statements about the need to support staff that are not backed up by policy or practice. It is essential that there is a genuinely supportive culture and not simply a set of empty proclamations that generate mistrust'
- well-being policies that are simply paper policies – that is, they exist on the shelf, but have no grounding in actual operational practices. In some ways this can be worse than having no policy at all, as the ill-feeling such tokenism can generate can be additional pressures for staff to have to contend with;
- relying solely on training to tackle stress issues. While training has an important role to play as part of an overall staff well-being strategy, it is not sufficient on its own, and can be counterproductive if awareness and expectations are raised without other measures to complement these. A focus on training can also contribute to pathologising – that is, reinforcing the idea that stress arises because of deficits on the part of individual employees.

I would therefore argue strongly that everyone involved should do all within their power to ensure that stress matters are given the serious attention they deserve, rather than treated tokenistically as a superficial response to a current fashion.

CONCLUSION

Investing in the future involves seeing stress in a more holistic way than the predominantly individual focus that is so often adopted. It involves everyone being 'stress aware' and taking seriously the harm that can be done by approaches to work (and wider life) pressures that blame the individual, ignore the crucial role of support and leave harmful processes and structures in place, untouched.

Stress is, to an organisation, what pain is to the human body – it is telling us that something is wrong somewhere, something needs attention and needs remedying. The more fully aware of this we are, the better equipped we will all be for rising to the challenges that stress presents without reducing this complex, multidimensional problem to a simple matter of personal inadequacy.

EXERCISE 14

The 'pain' analogy is a very useful one. It helps us to understand stress more holistically.

- How might you be able to use the understanding this analogy brings to make sense of your own experiences of pressure?
- What are its implications in terms of preventing and responding to stress?

Postscript for managers

A recurring theme here has been the emphasis on all members of an organisation being important stakeholders when it comes to dealing with stress matters. However, what also has to be recognised is that managers have an additional layer of responsibility. They are charged with not only managing their own pressures as effectively as possible, but also supporting their staff in managing theirs, by means of appropriate and constructive supervisory practices and, more broadly, through contributing to an organisational culture in which:

- stress is not seen simply as a sign of individual weakness or inadequacy;
- discussion of feelings, pressures, problems and mistakes is encouraged rather than suppressed or stigmatised;
- pressures are recognised and acknowledged, rather than swept under the carpet or ignored;
- people's efforts and achievements are valued, and appreciation is openly expressed; and
- coping methods are recognised, encouraged, fostered and enhanced.

This, of course, presents a significant challenge to managers, a set of pressures to add to all the others that come with the job description! But, challenges are also, potentially at least, major sources of job satisfaction and personal and professional rewards.

It is also important to be aware that it is a collective challenge, one that needs to be faced together – with other managers, with staff, and indeed with all involved in the organisation. Stress can have the effect of making people feel isolated – and even of making people isolate themselves – and so the importance of working together becomes even more of an imperative.

The law lays responsibility on organisations (and therefore managers) to protect their staff from undue hazards, including stress. There is, of course, also a moral or humanitarian duty to safeguard colleagues at all levels from the destructive effects of stress. The impetus to take stress matters seriously is therefore a strong one, and so the value of understanding stress and responding positively and constructively to it is clearly enormous.

Postscript for self-employed people

There has been much discussion in this manual about organisations, employers, management and so on; but, of course, much of that will not apply if you are self-employed. However, the basic principles will be the same, in the sense that we all need support; no one is entirely self-contained and fully independent.

So, the key question if you are self-employed is: Where do you get your support from? Informal support from friends and family can be invaluable, although it is important not to overload them (sadly, many marriages and other relationships have broken up because of work pressures being taken home).

It is therefore important to look more broadly for sources of support, such as the following.

- *A mentor or other trusted adviser.* Having the opportunity to talk through your pressures can be a very effective way of keeping those pressures in perspective, thereby preventing them reaching an unmanageable level.
- *One or more networking groups.* Networking is not just about getting referrals.
- *Being part of a supportive group* where you are made to feel welcome and are valued can make a big difference. They also provide the opportunity to discuss shared problems and challenges.
- *Business support systems* offered by local councils or other governmental bodies have the potential to serve as sources of support too.
- *Online support* can be helpful in some circumstances – for example, if you are a member of an online learning community or similar.

Whatever source(s) of support you choose to use, the key point is that it is essential that you are aware of the support possibilities available to you and are prepared to use them, rather than leave yourself vulnerable to stress by trying to soldier on alone. Running your own business can be extremely rewarding, but we have to be aware too that it brings considerable demands and challenges, and it would be naïve to think that stress is something that happens to other people, not to us.

Postscript for tutors and trainees

This manual can be used to accompany an in-service training course or college or university module. In particular, the practice focus illustrations could be used as a basis for discussion. Similarly, the exercises at the end of each chapter have been designed with individual study in mind. However, it would not take much adaptation to convert them into group exercises.

Sources of support

Employing organisations have a duty of care under health and safety legislation to safeguard their employees from undue hazards – and that includes stress. Therefore, in principle at least, there should be help and support available in house.

In addition, the following organisations offer information and/or guidance in relation to stress and related matters:

Mind (UK)
Mind mental health charity provides information and support for all aspects of mental health and well-being – www.mind.org.uk/

Mental Health Foundation (UK and Ireland)
The Mental Health Foundation is another mental health charity that offers information and resources on mental health and well-being – www.mentalhealth.org.uk/

Samaritans (UK & Ireland)
A charity offering emotional support providing 24/7 confidential emotional support – www.samaritans.org/. The Samaritans Helpline at 116 123 is available free of charge 24/7.

Shout 85258
A text service for mental health support (text SHOUT to 85258).

Anxiety UK
A charity offering support for people struggling with anxiety issues – www.anxietyuk.org.uk/

Minding Your Head (Northern Ireland)
Information and support for mental health in Northern Ireland – www.mindingyourhead.info/

NB Trade unions and professional associations also have a key role to play in preventing stress and in supporting their members when they face stress-related challenges.

References

Arroba, T and James, K (1987) *Pressure at Work: A Survival Guide*. New York: McGraw-Hill.

Bevan, S and Cooper, C L (2022) *The Healthy Workforce: Enhancing Wellbeing and Productivity in the Workers of the Future*. Bingley: Emerald Publishing.

Bono, E de (1991a) *Atlas of Management Thinking*. Harmondsworth: Penguin.

Bono, E. de (1991b) *Masterthinker's Handbook: A Guide to Innovative Thinking*. Harmondsworth: Penguin.

Cheese, P (2021) *The New World of Work: Shaping a Future that Helps People, Organizations and Our Societies to Thrive*. London: Kogan Page.

Croner-i (2024) Stress at Work: In-depth. [online] Available at: app.croneri.co.uk/topics/stress-work/indepth?product=133 (accessed 4 April 2024).

Fried, J and Heinemeier Hansson, D (2013) *Remote: Office Not Required*. London: Vermilion.

Health and Safety Executive (HSE) (2024) Work-related stress and how to manage it. [online] Available at: www.hse.gov.uk/stress/overview.htm#:~:text=HSE%20defines%20stress%20as%20'the,with%20pressures%20and%20other%20issues (accessed 4 April 2024).

Maslach, C and Jackson, S (1981) *The Maslach Burnout Inventory*. Palo Alto, CA: Psychology Consulting Press/London: Routledge.

Matud, M (2004) Gender Differences in Stress and Coping Styles. *Personality and Individual Differences*, 37: 1401–15.

May, V M (2015) *Pursuing Intersectionality: Unsettling Dominant Imaginaries*. New York: Routledge.

More, W (1997) *The New A-B-C of Handling Aggression*. Birmingham: PEPAR Publications.

Schön, D (1983) *The Reflective Practitioner*. London: Temple.

Thompson, N (2018) *Promoting Equality: Working with Diversity and Difference*, 4th edn. London: Bloomsbury.

Thompson, N (2021) *People Skills*, 5th edn. London: Bloomsbury.

Thompson, N (2022) *The Loss and Grief Practice Manual*. Wrexham: Avenue Media Solutions.

Thompson, N (2024a) *Effective Problem Solving*, 2nd edn. St Albans: Critical Publishing.

Thompson, N (2024b) *Authentic Leadership Revisited*, 2nd edn. Cheltenham: Edward Elgar.

Thompson, N and Gilbert, P (2019) *Reflective Supervision: A Learning and Development Manual*, 2nd edn. Brighton: Pavilion.

Thompson, N and McGowan, J (2024) *How to Survive in Social Work*, 2nd edn. London: Jessica Kingsley Publishers.

Thompson, N, Stradling, S, Murphy, M and O'Neill, P (1996) Stress and Organisational Culture. *British Journal of Social Work*, 26(5), 647–65. doi.org/10.1093/oxfordjournals.bjsw.a011139.

Milton Keynes UK
Ingram Content Group UK Ltd.
UKHW020629050724
445059UK00002B/6

9 781916 925342